Praise for *Stories from th* *Pain, Betrayal, and Resilience, on th*

"I have known Lisa since we were classmates at the A ⌐₋ₐᵢₗ Course in 1993. We were colleagues. We sat next to each other in assigned seating during every auditorium session. I got to know her. I saw her as a hardnosed professional who didn't take crap from anyone. She held her own and projected a high level of confidence that, honestly, I wish I had.

"It wasn't until I read this book that I gained a full appreciation of what Lisa and many other women and victims of military sexual trauma endured. As a man reading Lisa's book, you will be challenged to assess your part in the scourge of MST. Are you one of the perpetrators who contributed to the misery of your female comrades in arms? Did you passively watch the wrongs being committed, but did nothing to stop it? Or were you operating just below the radar, riding the fence-line of what was and what was not appropriate behavior, not really caring about the perspective of your targeted victim?

"My advice to all who read this book: Read it, digest it, and become an advocate of immediate change for all our warriors so they can focus 100 percent on the grim, vital business of warfighting. Lisa Carrington Firmin's book is a call to arms."

—**Lieutenant Colonel R. B. Crosson**, U.S. Army (Retired),
UH-60, AH-1, OH-58, UH-1 Master Army Aviator,
recently retired Chief Operating Officer, deBoer Transportation

"As a woman veteran, I must say that *Stories from the Front* was a difficult read, but it is a MUST READ. Going from chapter to chapter knowing and understanding that any of these women could have been me during my four years of active-duty service is horrifying. Some people will never understand the desire to serve, and what makes a woman veteran continue to do so after being sexually harassed and, for some, raped while in uniform is beyond noble. *Stories from the Front* does a remarkable job of showing how heroic women veterans are even after being propelled into a battlefield within the battlefield of military sexual assault!"

—**Ginger Miller**, U.S. Navy veteran
President and CEO, Women Veterans Interactive

"Invaluable effort to capture the extreme personal side of military sexual trauma in all its forms, and a must-read for armed forces leaders at all levels. There are tragic life-altering stories herein, but success stories as well. The common denominator in all of them is leadership. It is my hope leaders will read these stories and hear these voices that echo from the Vietnam era to the current day, and look at their own organizations. Young leaders, what is tolerated? The behaviors you accept are the standards you set. Senior leaders, look at where and how these stories took place; how do you know what is happening in your areas of responsibility and what actions have you taken — beyond a policy letter — to crush conditions that allow an environment where these events happen? We should all be grateful for the courage of these service members in telling their stories, and for Colonel Firmin's outstanding efforts to deliver them in a caring and compassionate way."

—Major General Tony Cucolo, U.S. Army (Retired)

"Lisa Carrington Firmin has exposed an arc of injustice in the military that has transcended time, gender, and ethnicity. Firmin exposes a dark cancer in the American military of sexual harassment and assault. Deftly weaving together heartbreaking stories of over a dozen survivors, including her own, Firmin's book tells the decades-long struggle of service men and women seeking justice. One will have no doubt after reading these powerful vignettes that disbelief and retaliation are the two hallmarks of the military's struggle to care for those serving this country. The book should be required reading for all generals and admirals tasked with leading the men and women who serve under them."

—Colonel Don Christensen, U.S. Air Force (Retired)
President, Protect Our Defenders

"My dominant emotion after reading these stories is admiration and respect for these veteran and military storytellers. I question how many other people would have the strength of heart and character, given the adversity and wounds they experienced, to forge ahead. By forging ahead, they succeeded; and by succeeding, they triumphed, each one of them. Ultimately this is an uplifting series of stories."

—Jeb Wyman, author of
What They Signed Up For: True Stories by Ordinary Soldiers

"Colonel Lisa Carrington Firmin has opened a door with this anthology, providing much-needed space for veterans to describe their experiences of harassment, intimidation, and sexual assault. All served their country honorably, with some being decorated combat veterans. Their stories raise so many questions. How is it that these veterans found few, if any, allies within their own ranks? How can the Uniform Code of Military Justice (UCMJ) overlook blatant crimes against soldiers, airmen, sailors, coasties, and Marines on active duty? How can their peers witness such behavior and turn a blind eye? Yet, toward the end of her own story of assault and retaliation, Col. Firmin puts an even more important question to her audience: what is the true cost of service to one's country? That question will require all of us, men and women alike, to confront some unpleasant truths."

—**Jeff Gatlin**, MS, LPC-S, U.S. Air Force veteran
licensed professional counselor-supervisor

"This important book needs to be read widely to understand the impact and affect change in our armed forces. The systemic issues in the military that ignore accountability and justice for people serving, or who have served, who have experienced sexual assault and harassment must end. With courage and care, the stories expose the devastating impact of military sexual trauma to service members and veterans of different eras, branches, races, and intersecting identities. Through the narratives within, the book also gives voice to the many of us with similar military experiences. This is a difficult and necessary read for us all, and particularly for military leadership and civilians to implement and advocate for changes that are long overdue. Thank you all for your courage in telling your experiences of betrayal and sexual assault in the military to help end a decades long pattern of minimizing and ignoring these issues and their effects."

—**Dr. Vanessa Meade**, PsyD, LCSW, U.S. Army Gulf War veteran

"Lisa's book is a true testament to her authentic voice and her ability to share her experiences in the military and assist others in sharing their own MST experiences."

—**Jenny Pacanowski**, U.S. Army veteran
Founder and Director, Women Veterans Empowered and Thriving

"These are terrifying accounts of the incredible journey of seclusion, gender discrimination, harassment, abuse, and sexual assault against our men and women serving in our armed forces. To know that these horrors came from our own against our own is unthinkable. By telling these stories, La Coronela shows a great determination for survival, resilience, dedication, and commitment to the sacred oath she took. Stepping up now to help others, she captures the lived experiences of MST survivors, in hopes of helping many women and men who served, are serving, and will serve. Such cruelty and atrocities must no longer be ignored in our U.S. military!"

—**Lupita Colmenero**, Chief Operating Officer, LATINA Style, Inc., Founder, Parents Step Ahead Inc., Publisher, *El Hispano News*

Stories from the Front

Pain, Betrayal, and Resilience
on the MST Battlefield

Lisa Carrington Firmin

BLUE EAR BOOKS

Published in 2022 by
Blue Ear Books
7511 Greenwood Ave N, Box 400
Seattle, WA 98103
USA

www.blueearbooks.com

ISBN: 978-0-9990951-9-5

Cover design: Kait Glasswell
Interior photographs provided by individuals in each chapter and digitally converted to black and white by Pete Sabo
Author back cover photograph by Matt Roberts
Page design: Jennifer Haywood, Blue Ear Books

For my sisters and brothers in arms who have been sexually harassed and/or sexually assaulted in the military, I stand with you.

For my family and friends who unconditionally surround me with love and support, familia es todo.

Trigger Warning

The subject matter of this book is military sexual trauma: sexual harassment, sexual assault, and rape. Additionally, there are some stories that deal with the reality of combat. The stories depicted in this book can be triggering for some individuals. Please refer to Appendix I for resources and organizations that can assist, or call the Veterans Crisis Line at 1-800-273-8255.

Definitions of Military Sexual Trauma, Sexual Harassment, and Sexual Assault

The following definition is from the United States Department of Veterans Affairs (VA):

Military Sexual Trauma is the term commonly used by the VA referring to assault or battery of a sexual nature and sexual harassment experiences that occur during military service.

For additional information, contact the VA:
https://www.mentalhealth.va.gov/msthome

The following definitions are from the United States Department of Defense Sexual Assault Prevention and Response Office (SAPR):

Sexual Harassment is a form of sex discrimination that involves unwelcome sexual advances, requests for sexual favors, and other verbal and physical acts of a sexual nature. Examples can include verbal comments, obscene or sexually explicit media contact, non-verbal actions, physical touching, and unwanted requests to perform sexual acts or sexual favors.

Sexual Assault is intentional sexual contact characterized by use of force, threats, intimidation, abuse of authority or when a victim does not or cannot consent. Examples can include rape, forcible sodomy (oral or anal), other unwanted sexual contact that is aggravated, abusive, or wrongful to include unwanted and inappropriate sexual contact or attempts to commit these acts.

For additional information contact DoD SAPR:
www.sapr.mil

Author's Note

Each story depicted in this book is factual to the best of everyone's recollection. However, the identity of some individuals described has been obscured to ensure privacy.

CONTENTS

GETTING HELP

FOREWORD

Stories from the Front is a brutally honest recounting by fourteen individuals who have experienced various forms of military sexual trauma (MST) in all branches of service, from harassment to assault to rape. It is a harrowing read, but I encourage you to soak up each story. Only then can you truly begin to comprehend the insidious nature of MST. It impacts much more than the individual who was subjected to the abuse; it digs deep and spreads its roots out across the personal as well as professional lives of individuals. It affects workplaces, coworkers, supervisors, extended family, spouses, and children. It spreads like a contagion, with nothing left untouched. Not only can the lives of the survivors be decimated, but the very mission of the military is negatively impacted by MST.

There are several recurring themes in each story told, but I found three to be the most salient. The first, MST has been a longstanding problem, as evidenced by the span of time covered by the stories: fifty years, from the Vietnam era to the present day. The stories clearly delineate the damage MST has done, and continues to do, not only to individuals, but to the military's strategic mission.

The second theme is that these stories collectively send a powerful message to those who have experienced MST, that they are not alone and not to blame. *Stories from the Front* includes stories from officers, enlisted personnel, veterans, active duty, people of color, thirteen women, one man, members of the LGBTQ community, disabled vets, and those who served in combat. It will surely resonate with many. MST can and does affect *anyone*. We can no longer hide from that fact.

The third theme is that there are indeed resources to help those who have experienced MST. However, we all must work harder to ensure that these resources are provided in a safe and non-triggering manner, both within the Department of Defense and the Department of Veterans Affairs and throughout the country's behavioral health community. The days of blaming and shaming victims of MST must end.

What saddens me so is that in 2004, I stood up the Department of Defense's first-ever Joint Task Force for Sexual Assault Prevention and Response and, although some progress has been made, it isn't nearly enough. DoD has been trying to eradicate MST for years without success. These stories speak of the failure to adequately assess the true nature of MST, the lack of dignity exhibited time and time again when dealing with survivors, and the inability to tackle MST within the ranks or to achieve any semblance of justice for victims and survivors.

With the recent passage of the 2021 National Defense Authorization Act, which includes sweeping changes to how sexual assault and sexual harassment are handled within the military, we are hopefully on the brink of real change. These changes promise to be transformational to the military justice system and to break the scourge of MST. However, it will require commitment, engagement, and focus from *all* levels of the DoD to ensure this promise is fully and finally realized.

Colonel Lisa Carrington Firmin provides much-needed insight into MST. The honest and compassionate way she tells her own story, and those of the others, illustrates the pain and betrayal each experienced, but also shouts of their resilience to survive and thrive. Their courage in speaking up now is to be commended. It is my hope that we learn from each story and vow to never again turn our backs on our sisters and brothers who served. Each of them took the oath to defend our country, and it is time that we pay that back by defending them and all who have suffered such personal indignities.

Major General KC McClain, U.S. Air Force (Ret.)
Former Commander, DoD Joint Task Force for Sexual Assault
Prevention and Response

Into the Light
by Lisa Carrington Firmin

While the world raged against a pandemic in 2020, the first in 100 years,

 I raged against a virulent strain of testosterone-filled traumas.

While the country masked up and used antibacterial sanitizer to keep the virus at bay,

 I lifted the mask that hid years of sexual harassment while serving my country.

While the nation underwent lockdowns and faced months of darkness to protect its citizens from the virus,

 I came into the light, face to face with the betrayals of my fellow brothers in arms.

While scientists researched innovative new vaccines,

 I reflected on my past military time serving alongside both professionals and hidden predators, and researched ways to heal.

While businesses tried to keep people six feet apart to be safe,

 I began learning how to let people in, closer to a heart and body that is guarded.

While most were wary and complained about isolation and quarantine,

 I felt safe hunkered down alone.

While I missed my family terribly,

 I used the lockdown and self-isolation to begin the long road of healing that had eluded me in the past.

While some courageously speak openly about military sexual trauma,

> I could not do that until one day in 2020 after a young Army Specialist was found brutally murdered on a military base.

While Vanessa Guillén anguished over reporting her sexual harassment and the retaliation it might bring,

> I understood all too well the trepidation and fear of what reporting my own could have brought.

While Vanessa's death astounded the country,

> I was affected deep into my Latina soul and her murder became a catalyst to acknowledge my own bitter truth.

While Vanessa's family mourned and demanded answers from an inept military,

> I found my voice from their tragic loss.

While the investigation into her murder revealed serious gaps within the military,

> I discovered my own repressed memories.

While sexually assaulted in initial training,

> I froze, tolerating more than anyone should ever have to.

While relentlessly harassed early in my career,

> I will not allow those early years to define me, I am a leader, a woman, a Latina, a combat warrior, my bronze star shines bright.

While other voices cry out for change within the Armed Services,

> I join them, my mask now lifted and walk into the light.

Written in April 2021

4

Stories

CHAPTER 1

Us vs. Her

Lisa Carrington Firmin

What scares me more than anything is that I don't remember everything he did to me. Will I ever, or has my brain protected me by allowing me to remember only the parts that I can handle? Maybe the worst would just be too much. It's scary not to know, not to remember all the details. And it's even scarier to remember.

He showed me a photograph of his wife, in a black negligee that left little to the imagination. She was a real looker, simply gorgeous. This was the man who was relentlessly sexually harassing me and had just recently upped his game to what I would later come to know as sexual assault. I remember thinking, "Why is he showing me this?" I just couldn't understand what his interest was in me. He was an instructor. I was a trainee, a scrawny young Latina trying to keep my head down, to survive long enough to graduate from officer training school (OTS).

Why would he want to mess around with me when he had that sexy, beautiful wife waiting for him at home? I did not understand then that his behavior was not about sex but about power. And boy, did he have power over me. He was one of our military training instructors, and one recommendation from him that I wasn't a good fit for the military is all it would have taken for me to get kicked out. If that happened, I could kiss a career as an officer goodbye. I had no Plan B. I wanted to be the first in my family to become an officer in the military, just as I had been the first to complete college.

Back then, in 1980, OTS was a thirteen-week program for college graduates, and when you graduated you were commissioned as a second lieutenant. There were lots of men, few women, even fewer Latinas. I don't think I ever saw someone who looked like me. We officer trainees were sometimes referred to on graduation as ninety-day wonders. I had no idea just how much of a wonder I was going to have to be. OTS consisted of learning Air Force customs, standards, history, leadership, team building, communications, drill & ceremonies, physical training, small arms training, field exercises, and more. To graduate we had to meet or exceed physical, academic, and military bearing standards. It was a very competitive and stressful environment.

The infrastructure and system at OTS stacked the deck against trainees. That was purposeful. They wanted to root out the weaker ones so they would quit or be kicked out. Whiners need not apply. Only the best survived and could begin careers as officers. We were to be possible leaders in combat; there was no room for indecisiveness or error. The training had to be tough, I knew that. But the infrastructure gave way too much power to training instructors. They told us when to get up in the morning, when to eat, when to do PT (physical training), when to study, when to do anything really. It enabled the predators among them to go rogue, to treat trainees with disrespect, harassment, and even sexual assault, all under the guise of effective training for real-world military scenarios. There were no real checks and balances for this, and at times I actually questioned (in my head, of course) whether the hazing and harassment were all part of the training.

Unfortunately for me, I stood out from the beginning because I was different. I was the wrong gender, too young (the youngest in the entire cohort), and somewhat of a smartass. And I was the wrong ethnicity. The lead training instructor reminded me constantly of how I didn't fit in. The instructors picked on me relentlessly. In initial training they try to break you, but these guys were really trying to break me so I would quit. People all around me were either quitting or getting kicked out for failure to meet standards. I was determined not to be one of them.

I held my own in training, was always in uniform or in the PT uniform, didn't wear makeup, downplayed my femininity, tried to be invisible when certain predators were around, which unfortunately was impossible because while going through officer training one had to stand out as a leader. It was as much about mind games as about physicality and military leadership.

There were some instructors and staff who gave me "that look" for just being there. I got picked on a lot due to my gender, age, and ethnicity. I was told that I was to get extra scrutiny and that I wouldn't be allowed to go off base for personal leave for a very long time. They lived up to that; as I recall, I was the last one in my flight (unit of about fourteen individuals) to get authorized weekend time off the base. Unlike my flight mates, I would repeatedly get excessive demerits for ridiculous things. I remember standing at attention or at parade rest for specific events or just waiting to meet with the flight commander, a second lieutenant, and being singled out, pointed at, and even touched under the guise of "Come look at how these women's uniforms fit." I was seething while standing there, but I couldn't break out of formation or position, as that would be against the rules, and I would end up suffering for it. So I clenched my jaw, bore down, and at times even bit my own tongue until it bled so I wouldn't blurt out exactly what I was thinking. In my head I was screaming for them to get their hands off me and that they could all go to hell. I think I even spoke ill of their mothers too. Never out loud, always in my head.

A particular training instructor began to target me. First just staring, waiting for me to screw up and make mistakes that he could call me out on. Then the eye fuckery really began, the leering, catcalls, you know how men undress women with their eyes: like that, but worse. And he did this stuff when no one else was around. He progressed from making remarks about my body, intimidating me about my ability to complete the training to become an officer, about how powerful he was, or how he could derail my chances to commission. I was so intimidated by his position of power over whether I would make it out of training. Then I got scared when he progressed from saying things to actually doing things to me: unwanted advances, kissing, grabbing, groping, and fondling.

He would come to my barracks room under pretense of an inspection or whatever he wanted and throw me against the bunkbeds. No one questioned him. He had a right to be there; it was his job. I was just a trainee, a nobody. I froze. I don't recall even screaming in my head, I was so totally shocked. It was as if this was happening to someone else. My mind couldn't comprehend it. I thought I was a strong person. I was overpowered and outmaneuvered. My roommate had already been kicked out and, for all I knew, the same thing had happened to her. I was barely twenty-one years old and being assaulted and harassed where I lived and worked. I just shut down and compartmentalized so I could survive training and get my commission.

It never entered my mind to report him. To whom would I have reported it? There were no formal reporting structures in place at all for this type of behavior. The power differential was enormous. This man was like a supernatural being in that place, and he knew it and flaunted it. Besides, no one would believe me.

I heard him before I saw him. I distinctly remember dreading the sound of the military taps he wore on his boots. Lots of military drill and training instructors wore them, supposedly to keep the heels from wearing out too soon. Really it was to intimidate us. When I heard the tap, tap, tap of his every step, I knew he was getting closer to me. My reaction was Pavlovian; anticipating his arrival brought such emotion and physical reactions. There was absolute quiet, then there was his tap, tap, tap. As soon as I heard the tap or saw him, I tensed up. My jaw clenched; I became like stone. Was he coming in as friend or foe? Would he be coming in his official status, to inspect my room, to discuss something military-related like PT, marching, small arms training? Or would he be coming to satisfy some strange obsession he had with me? Why had he sought me out? I asked myself this over and over again. I wasn't the weak one in the herd, but I became a conquest to be sought out and conquered by this predator. I was his prey, his trophy.

None of these thoughts ultimately mattered as to why I was singled out, but to me, back then, they consumed me. What was so difficult about going through this very intense training, while trying to keep him away from me, was that to get through I had to stand out. I already had three strikes against me: I was young, I was a woman, and I was a Latina. I was being reminded of this lack of conformity, being different, every day.

I had no idea just how deeply I had buried what happened to me at OTS all those years ago, or how well I had learned to compartmentalize negative aspects of my military career, until a young Army Specialist named Vanessa Guillén was murdered on April 22, 2020.

The dam started to break loose and repressed memories flooded into my head, shaking me up. Imagine totally forgetting that this had happened to you in initial training. I had buried it so deeply that even now, as I undergo therapy and try to work through it all, it's almost as if it happened to someone else. It couldn't have happened to me, right? Forty years later, I still have problems remembering exactly what occurred during the incidents involving this instructor. I see only fragments, bits and pieces that are fleeting, floating around in my head. It's like trying to watch an old Super 8mm movie that has been spliced and cut so many times that you are never able to watch it from start to end, there are just too many gaps. I try to grasp them so I can understand exactly what happened, but they slip through, elusively hiding in my mind, probably salvaging my sanity. My default is to not remember, to let the memories stay buried. I ask myself: Was I complicit in some way? What I wore, what I said, how I carried myself? I try to rationalize that all that doesn't matter, I was a trainee undergoing what I would call a form of brainwashing, totally vulnerable to the leadership in that training environment. I probably would have done whatever they asked me to do. In just a few short weeks, I came to bleed Air Force blue and was totally committed to serving my country. Someone took advantage of all that and violated my humanity. Then the shame, guilt, and embarrassment hit me hard, screaming at me about why I never said anything to anyone then or later, or that I need to try harder to remember.

What scares me more than anything is that I don't remember everything he did to me. Will I ever, or has my brain protected me by allowing me to remember only the parts that I can handle? Maybe the worst would just be too much. It's scary not to know, not to remember all the details. And it's even scarier to remember.

So how did a young Latina make her way to OTS? That's easy: My father served in both the Navy and the Air Force and always told me that joining the military after college would be a good option, as I could come in as an officer and lead. He knew that I wanted to lead. My father retired as an E-7, a master sergeant, and wanted his children to do better, be better. My family is from South Texas, what we affectionately call *el valle*, the valley. We are proud Latinos, proud Texicans, proud Mexican Americans. We come from solid stock where each generation has a love of country and God instilled into them along with a solid work ethic, to always be as good as your word. I learned early on that what one says matters. We were taught the Ten Commandments; we knew what was right and what was wrong.

My parents never had the opportunity to graduate from high school. They had to work very hard to ensure their families had enough resources just to survive. My mother came from a family of ten and had to drop out of high school in ninth grade, after her mother passed away, to work as well as take care of her siblings. Her youngest sibling was just a year old. This was just what was done back then, and particularly within our Latino culture. My father ended up getting a GED so he could join the military, after taking on lower-level jobs and not reaching much success. I have three degrees, worked in higher education after the military, and to this day often say that my parents were two of the smartest people I have known. They had graduate degrees from the school of hard knocks.

I knew I had to go to college; my dad told me so every day. He kept saying, "You will be the first generation in our family to go to college." But since we had no college people in our family, no one was around to prepare us. There was no college track program in our high school, at least not for us. There were many obstacles, not the least of which was my father's massive stroke when I was in ninth grade. It was devastating to our family. We had just adopted my younger sister and brother from Costa Rica. They were

14

not yet legally part of the family, and the red tape seemed insurmountable. And now our vibrant, athletic father was lying in a military hospital bed in the United States fighting for his life, and we were stuck back in Panama, where he had been stationed. He just happened to be in the States going through some preretirement actions.

I'm not sure if he would have lived if he had been in Panama when the stroke happened and when a second one occurred while he was in the hospital. He was quickly transferred by helicopter to Wilford Hall Hospital at Lackland Air Force Base in San Antonio, and there he remained for six months. My mother was told he might not live, and that she should return to the States immediately. All us kids stayed in Panama with our extended military family, who took great care of us. The outstanding way the military family rallied around us was probably another reason I later joined up. Waiting across the ocean, away from our mother, was extremely difficult and rocked the stability and continuity of my world.

The immediate problem was that we could not legally take our new sister and brother out of Panama, because the paperwork wasn't done yet. Many people told my mother, "Just stop the adoption. Take the kids back to Costa Rica and go to your husband in the States." She absolutely rejected this and endured countless problems trying to get the adoption expedited. She held steady and never wavered. My mother's steadfastness typified her selfless foundation of always doing for others and doing the right thing, no matter how hard it is.

We finally were able to leave Panama as an entire family. When I first saw my father after six months, I did not recognize him. He was a shell of his former self. It took several years for my faith in God to be fully restored. My mother's faith never lessened, despite how extremely difficult it was for her to take care of a paraplegic and four kids.

When I walked into my new civilian high school I looked like a Latina, but according to my classmates I didn't act or talk like one. They immediately rejected me. They thought I acted stuck up or something. I had grown up all over the world, gone to Department of Defense schools, lived on military bases among cultures unlike my own. I had the lived experience of learning about diversity and inclusion, long before it came in vogue.

Starting after the school year had begun was a shock to me for several reasons, not only because we were dealing with a very ill father who was learning to walk and talk again. We were uprooted, didn't even have our belongings; those were back in Panama. We were learning to live with our new sister and brother, teaching them things about the family, helping teach them English, trying to get them to trust us. We couldn't afford a house yet, so we lived with relatives until things settled down and we knew whether our father could come home. Except we had no home. Things were extremely difficult for us, and then throw in a new school with all its cliques. I recall soon after arriving one Latina picking on me and demanding that I meet her after school to fight. I was terrified, hardly knew anyone, but was being treated cruelly just because I was different. I showed up, she never did, and I breathed a huge sigh of relief. My older brother and I ended up hanging out with the jocks since we really didn't fit in anywhere else. The Latinos, whites, Blacks, potheads, country folks, bandmates, no group claimed or wanted us. I was too Latino for the whites, not Latina enough for the Latinos.

It was a strange time for me. I was just glad that the athletes and coaches welcomed us. That's when I learned that talent could open doors and provide opportunities, that to be part of a team meant I had to pull my weight too, that no one was successful unless we all worked together. I had a great basketball coach who taught the team so much. These were lifelong lessons. I did end up making some great friends during high school, lifelines at a time when my life was in upheaval. They probably have no idea how much they meant to me back then. I'm so grateful to have these friends still in my life.

The pressure to complete high school and go on to college was always there, even more so after my father's strokes. I felt the weight of my family's future on me, but I just didn't know enough about college to really prepare myself in high school. I played basketball, wrote for the school newspaper, and was involved in clubs, but never really worked hard at academics. I coasted and never really challenged myself. I shouldn't have been surprised when a guidance counselor told me that I should consider vocational school. That was a wake-up call. Okay, so I was not prepared. But I knew I could do it.

My *ganas* kicked in. *Ganas* is a Spanish word for desire or ambition. In college, I was determined to be the first in my family to graduate. I couldn't wait to get out and make my mark on the world. After my first year of college, I realized I was wasting time during the summer working at minimum-wage jobs, and that if I went to school year-round, I could get out sooner. So that is what I did.

My father used to say that his stroke "was a blessing in disguise and had a silver lining." No way could he have afforded to send all his kids to college on an enlisted man's retirement. Within a year he was medically retired and rated 100 percent disabled by the Department of Veterans Affairs. All his dependents could attend college with funding from the VA. Leave it to my rock-solid parents to find a silver lining. I had no excuse but to go to college and get out as soon as I could, especially when that silver lining covered so much of my expenses, since I had attended a public institution that was affordable.

Besides, I had real motivation. Not only did I want to be first in the family to graduate, but I really wanted to beat my brother to that finish line. He was a year older, but we were in the same grade; I caught up with him in fourth grade and never looked back. We were extremely competitive, in sports, in garnering our parents' approval, in just about everything. He was a much better athlete than I was, and we probably were evenly matched academically. Please don't tell him I said that.

I graduated in three years with honors and became the first in our family ever to complete college. That first college degree completely changed the trajectory of our family tree. College wasn't easy, as I had no one to guide me, but I muddled through. I met some great people at Texas A&I University (now known as Texas A&M Kingsville). It was small, and I could have discussions with faculty at any time. The people there looked a lot like me and were happy I was there. My college roommate became my best friend and is still paramount in my life. Those years at A&I were ones of introspection, real critical thinking, and learning. It was a great school for me.

So, I liked it a lot, but my first semester was a disaster. I was only seventeen and on my own for the first time. I partied, skipped class, and drank a lot. After that first semester, I did a gut check and figured out what I needed to do: Go to class. Study. Do the homework and engage with my professors. Who knew that was the secret sauce to completion? I found that I really was a lot smarter than most people thought I was. This wasn't the first time I had been underestimated, and it certainly wouldn't be the last.

Immediately after college, I started work on a graduate degree and worked part time. Quickly I realized that everyone in my graduate program brought several years, if not a lifetime, of work experience to the classroom. I was twenty years old. I had only worked briefly at minimum wage jobs and had experience with internships and volunteer work, but I found myself unable to contribute significantly in the classroom. I decided to drop out of grad school and get work experience and be the leader I knew I could be by joining the military. A few years later this decision was validated, as I had *mucho* to contribute attending a graduate program at night and on weekends while on active duty. I could translate my military leadership experiences directly to a master's program in organizational theory and human resource management.

After initial training I went to my technical school for two months, then landed at my first assignment: an all-male fighter pilot training squadron. Back then, women were not allowed to be fighter pilots. I was the first woman officer and first Latina they had seen, and for that I got more than my share of crap dished out daily.

At this first assignment, I experienced all forms of sexual harassment and gender discrimination, from offensive, threatening, and humiliating images, gestures, and language, to behaviors that left me totally isolated. All the officers outranked me; I was a brand-new second lieutenant. The enlisted personnel had years of experience on me. I had to prove myself, all while being subjected to this disgraceful behavior. Back then I didn't even know the term "toxic workplace," but I was living it.

I remember early in my career being asked if I was going to be a Bitch or a Whore. No one ever asked the men in the unit these types of questions. I often wondered: Why are those my only choices, and who said I have to choose? When forced to choose, I always chose Bitch. Who wants to be a Whore? I know the few other women who served when I did were asked these same questions. But sometimes they were given a third option: Dyke.

Days into my time there, something caught my eye at the entrance to the large auditorium where the pilots received their academic training. Every fourth or fifth slide was a centerfold from *Penthouse* or *Hustler* magazine – explicit female genitalia up close and in your face, on the large screen at the front of the auditorium.

When I spoke up about it, I was told it was the only way to hold the pilots' interest in the complex fighter pilot academic courses. This policy of showing "beaver shots" never changed throughout my time there, almost three years. I walked by that auditorium every day, sometimes multiple times. The men would see those pictures, then see me walking around the squadron. My opinion on seeing women objectified and demeaned never mattered. I was severely outnumbered, and no one cared what I thought or how this made me feel.

I never let them see me sweat, but back home I often cried in the shower. I felt so alone, and it was all so overwhelming. I had to decide: Was I going to stick with it or quit? In my family quitting is not an option, and I had taken an oath to serve. Plus, these men were not going to break me. Besides, I knew how much my serving meant to my father. I was the first woman and the first officer in our family to serve in the military. When I graduated from college, early mind you, my father said, "That's nice, Flaca." (The nickname means "skinny" in Spanish.) When I got my commission as a second lieutenant, he was so happy he cried. So I knew I had to stay in. I had to dig deep to gain the strength I needed just to survive, much less try to excel in this man's military.

I was constantly on the receiving end of repeated and unwanted sexual advances, literally asked out so often it became SOP, standard operating procedure. I finally got so fed up that one day I went on the squadron's intercom system and just blurted out: "Listen up, everyone. Please stop asking me out. I will not go out with any of you, ever." I shocked everyone, even myself. I had to learn to control my anger.

I could never just be me. I was constantly on guard, had to have eyes in the back of my head. A typical day entailed having at least a few men walking behind me in the hallways, gesturing wildly with their hands and hips, making seductive sexual gestures. When I turned around they would pretend they had done nothing. These were grown men. Many times, speaking to me, their eyes would land on my chest or lower. I would say, "Hey, I'm up here. Can we have a professional conversation?" I even started wearing uniform blouses that were too big for me, to try to hide my femininity. Nothing really helped.

The wives of the fighter pilots got in on the game too. At the first social party I was invited to, they looked me up and down and said, very sarcastically, "So you're the new lieutenant my husband works with now." I should have left then and there. Later in the evening, people got naked and jumped into the hot tub. I got teased by both men and women because I wouldn't participate. I went home.

I attended a few more parties before I realized that there was swinging going on, literally wife swapping. They would all put their house keys into a basket, then pick out one and end up with whoever that key belonged to. I stopped going to the parties.

You must understand that I was trying hard to fit in. I went to the parties thinking they were including me. Besides, my boss and the commander attended some of the parties and if you want to move up and get noticed, you need to make sure they know you and your work. I do recall that the really serious partying went on once the commander left. I represented women and Latinas, whether I wanted to or not, no matter where I was or what I was doing. That's heavy stuff to be laid on a 21-year-old. I learned the hard way that the parties were not really about work or professional development but were just another way women were demeaned and objectified.

I used to wonder if all the women who served in the Air Force got treated this way. Was it because I ended up in one of the most hypermasculine subcultures of the Air Force as my very first assignment? Or was it just me? And if it was me, why was it me? Because I was the first woman officer in that fighter squadron, or because I was a Latina, or because I was young, or what? It took years for me to realize that it wasn't me; it was always them. It was a culture that was toxic for women, a real playground of boy's club bullshit, and I just walked right into the middle of it.

Each day was a battle for respect, for my own sanity and oh, by the way, I was still trying to do my job and go to graduate school at night and on weekends. I compartmentalized and powered through. I knew they were just waiting to see the crack in my armor so they could say, "See, women should not be in the military."

Shortly after my arrival the unit (read the men) put up a sign that said *Us* and *Her*, with a line drawn vertically between the two. I was told it was so they could keep score on me versus the entire unit. Each day was a fight to see if I had made any progress, or what the sign reflected at week's end when the "scores" were tabulated. Did I win, did I lose, and what the hell did it matter? How did I get stuck in this petty game of one-upmanship surrounded by both junior- and senior-ranking pilots overflowing with testosterone?

Some of the more trivial but still disturbing hazing occurred when several pilots decided to take my desk apart. I had to search for hours, in different offices around the building, to find my desk drawers, then take even more time to put it all back together. It never mattered whether I had been working on some vital work that had a deadline. I had to come in many times after hours or on the weekends to get all my stuff back in its rightful place, just so I could do my job.

After a time, I had had it with these trivial hazing rituals. I'm not proud of it, but I struck back. I came in on a weekend when they weren't flying or around the squadron. I chose one pilot's desk and not only took out the drawers and dispersed them but moved the entire desk. I moved each drawer to a different office and put the desk in the hallway. I left him with a trash can, a piece of plexiglass on top of that, and a phone on top of that. As my father used to say, "How do you like them apples?"

The reaction on Monday was priceless. Strike a point for *Her* on the board. This is how it went for a long time, back and forth. At times they escalated, other times they deescalated, but they never stopped completely. I never forgot that I was the single *Her* and they were collectively the *Us*. It was mentally and physically exhausting. I am so sorry to say that after a while I normalized their behavior and even stooped to their level with my own retaliatory games. This was a survival mechanism on my part, a way to withstand the daily harassment and deal with the barrage of crap being dished out.

Life was always difficult, never easy. And, of course, it was easy to make me an "other" because I so clearly was. I was the first woman officer to dare enter their world, and the first Latina. I wasn't really one of them. I couldn't even be a fighter pilot. I don't think most of them even saw me as a fellow officer.

And this made it so much easier to treat me the way they did. Some men in the unit did not intentionally set out to demean me, but what did that matter? Their actions all landed on me like a ton of bricks, full weight, as if they had been premeditated, planned, and deliberate. Does it matter if it was a purposeful surgical strike or collateral damage? As the woman on the receiving end, it made no difference to me whether they were intentional or not. They still felt like deep cuts slowly killing me every day.

Those that were truly predatory and deliberate clearly showed that they enjoyed what they were doing. Those were the ones that really frightened me, as I wondered where on the continuum of harm they would draw the line.

They came close to crossing the line when they put a dead rat on my desk. They were looking to get a rise out of me, to see how horrified I would get. I disappointed them when I simply picked up the dead rat by its tail and threw it in the trash. By this time I had figured out that they were like narcissists, actively looking for reactions from me. Simply ignoring them was a good course of action that seemed to work for a while.

It was a hypermasculine culture not only in that first squadron I was assigned to but throughout the base, with a climate permissive of heavy drinking, sexual harassment, hazing, and gender, racial, and ethnic discrimination. This was pretty much how the entire service was back then, but it was that much more amped up in the fighter pilot world. Further, I was on the receiving end of jokes about being a spic, a beaner, and a wetback. One familiar joke was that I had swum across the Rio Grande with my belongings in a plastic bag on my head. These were cruel and insensitive and offended me much more than I ever let on.

Most of the fighter squadrons had lounges in their buildings where they would hang and drink. In my squadron, there was a urinal that had been converted to dispense beer on tap. Yup, that was my workplace. Alcohol flowed freely and often. You didn't even have to go to the officers' club to drink; it was right there in the building you worked in.

And I will admit that during these early years in the service I drank entirely too much and behaved in ways I shouldn't have. But these were part of my initial coping strategy to hang in there and do my job. I now understand that not only were these coping strategies harmful, but the behavior I exhibited was also directly attributable to what had happened to me in initial training. I acted this way in large measure because of my previous assault. Even though I had blocked it out and didn't even remember it, my brain and my body retained all that ugliness and trauma.

Some will say: What did you expect when you signed up? The military is well known as a male-dominated structure. Your first assignment was to a fighter squadron. You should not have been surprised at how you were treated. Well, I did not expect to be treated with contempt, sexually harassed at every turn. The fact that I did not have a penis should not have made me a target. I took the oath to serve and defend the Constitution, just like all the men did. We should have been viewed as equals. But it was the early 1980s, and women had just started to come into the military in larger numbers, although still not reaching anything close to critical mass. In fact, they still have not reached critical mass.

The percentage of women in the military when I joined was about 8.5 percent. Well into the 1980s, women constituted less than two percent of colonels and Navy captains. I had no role models to speak of. I did not even work for a woman until I had been in the military eighteen years, and that was briefly at the Pentagon, and it never happened again. And I never worked for a Hispanic or Latino officer. I served as my own role model, blazing trails I didn't even know I was blazing.

Many, both in and out of uniform, did not accept women in the military. In those early years, they were very overt and vocal about it. I felt like part of some giant experiment to prove women belonged and could lead, and that I had better not screw up. Both my gender and my ethnicity weighed heavy on me, as I knew all my mistakes would be magnified and could have negative impacts on others.

Many times during my first assignments, I was asked why I was so tall and why my name wasn't more ethnic. They had such terrible stereotypes about *mi gente*. They would say, "Carrington and Firmin just don't seem ethnic, you know?" I am Latina; my family names are Rivera, De La Rosa and Tamez. But Carrington really is my dad's last name, and he was definitely Latino. I won't bore you with all the genealogy. Let's just say I got many questions, was asked if I was Exotic, Eurasian, Filipino, or Indian. WTF is Exotic? I wasn't an animal to be hunted.

I am ashamed to admit that I downplayed not only my gender, but my ethnicity, especially at that first assignment. It wasn't until my second and subsequent assignments that I became more comfortable with my Latina heritage in uniform. Initially I tried to assimilate into the military and downplayed everything authentic about me, everything that made me who I really was. I so wanted to be like the white men in charge. The entire thirty years I served, I was never my whole authentic self. Do you know how exhausting that can be? I codeswitched constantly, acting and speaking one way at work, another at home, another with my Latino familia, and yet another with military friends and community leaders.

What I experienced at this first assignment, surrounded by males in flight suits, was not the "boys will be boys" mentality. It went much deeper and, in some cases, was more sinister. For a few of my male officers, it was predatory: "Let's see who can bed the first woman officer in the unit." I felt like I was being viewed as some kind of conquest, the newest piece of meat on display, and all the men were starving. I felt like I was the oasis in the desert. The sexual banter, sexual and ethnic jokes, gestures, sexual harassment, sexism, misogyny, bullying, hazing at this first assignment were unrelenting.

And it wasn't only the men who fostered this culture. I detested other service women who flaunted their sexuality, flirting, overly demonstrative in looking for a husband, batting their eyelashes, giggling, asking for help from the strong men. The second woman officer (after me) in the unit I had been assigned to told me, "I came in to marry a pilot, can't wait to find a husband." Another young woman officer sat on the bar at the officers' club and actively flirted with all the male officers. This infuriated me. How could they think their behavior was professional? No one would ever take them seriously. Typically, it would have the opposite effect.

These types of women gave a bad name to the rest of us who were trying every day to prove not only that we belonged but that we were good at our jobs. They lived up to every negative stereotype that most men had of women serving. Not only did I have to combat the belief from some of the men I served with and the larger public that women shouldn't serve, but I had to work twice as hard to dispel the neanderthal stereotypes that these unprofessional women had foisted on me and others.

I cannot believe that I stayed in after that first assignment. I wanted out of that squadron and off that base, so I volunteered for an extended tour overseas just to get out of there. I ended up staying on that base for three long years before my reassignment came through. No one really volunteers for long extended tours, because it means you will be sent to an overseas location (many times not of your choice) and stuck there for four long years. What if that place was worse? Could it really be worse? Fighter pilots were only one of the subcultures in the military. In my second assignment, I was going to find out about another one.

I ended up at a maintenance squadron in the Philippines, what was called an aircraft generation squadron or AGS. There were 700 personnel, ten of whom were women. I thought that was not too bad, especially since I was replacing another woman. I wasn't going to be the *first* again. This unit was on the flight line, and maintainers have a whole subculture themselves that I very quickly learned about. Let's just say that they are renowned for working hard and playing even harder. Their language is even more colorful than a sailor's.

I had a run-in with an E-8, a senior enlisted maintainer. He literally walked right up to me on the flight line one day soon after my arrival and said, "The flight line is no place for a woman. I'm gonna make your life hell until you quit." He was inches from my face as he said this, with more enthusiasm than was necessary. I held my ground, did not step back. He moved even closer, his nose almost touching mine. I said to him: "I don't give a shit how many friggin' stripes you have on your sleeve. You see that little bar on my shoulder? It means I outrank your ass, so back the fuck off."

I was being tested; I knew that. By holding my ground and not taking any crap from him, I crossed over into a new area. He still made my life a living hell, but I ended up with his respect, and others started seeing me as someone they shouldn't mess with. Every day was a fight for my dignity and self-respect. Daily life on the flight line was all too similar to what I had experienced in the fighter squadron, less sexual in nature but more gendered. I found it a bit easier to take.

But soon the unwanted sexual advances started up again: the leering, the catcalls. People showing up at my door when I went TDY (temporary duty away) and basically expecting sex. What goes TDY stays TDY, is what they would say. These were my fellow officers. I never opened the door, told them to get lost. I hated going TDY, began to dread it, as I knew what would happen. I would get propositioned by my fellow airmen and also by the men wherever we were temporarily working. These could be other service personnel, contractors, or foreign nationals. They all just expected sex.

One full colonel, when I was still a young captain, told me that I should not have joined the military; I should be a model, as I was just too pretty to serve. He leered at me a lot and made me very uncomfortable. He loved taking pictures with me when we were at the same events. I avoided these situations as much as possible, but ultimately it was my job to attend.

I used to travel with my own bathroom sign that said *Women* because none existed in many of the places I had to go. I got tired of having to go to another building or floor to use a female restroom, when there were so many male restrooms where I worked or lived. The sign didn't deter some men; they just walked right on in when my sign was on the door and I was inside. But once I got up in rank, people started keeping their distance. With rank I gained power and privilege, and the harassment went covert. The concept of Rank Has Its Privileges (RHIP) was alive and well.

Even with more rank, I still experienced microaggressions and sometimes explicit bias. For example, I was being excluded from what I call spheres of influence, like the golf course, officers' club, and selective events or special duties, where you could gain access to key leaders and influencers on a base. This was how the game of leadership was played in the military.

I had to forge my way into those spheres. At times it wasn't easy, but I forced it. I wasn't about to be excluded from an event, a game, or a lunch where leaders, typically white males, would informally gather to make key decisions. I wanted in and found ways to break through. Since I detested golf, I learned to shoot skeet and met with key leaders that way. I would show up at informal gatherings, listen in and learn, and speak up when necessary.

Many times, at a meeting or conference, I would be the only woman and Latina at the table. I noticed that when I said something, no one reacted, but five minutes later a white man would say the same thing and be rewarded with sounds of praise for his great idea. I would stand up, literally stand up, and say, "Excuse me, but I said that five minutes ago. It was my idea. Let's just set the record straight, please." This happened more times than I can say. My standing up was intentional, and it was also shocking. Most people, certainly most minority women, did not speak up. I had learned years before to pick my battles and not to let some comments go.

When I was pregnant, I didn't tell my boss for five and a half months. I thought he was going to fire me, and he could have. I was an executive officer for a very demanding general officer. I just bought uniforms that were larger and kept on working those long hours. You would think he would have figured it out, as I was eating cheeseburgers at my desk at 0600. It was dumb, of course, for me to work that hard and long while pregnant, but I was trying to prove that women could do it all. When I finally did tell him, I asked that he not treat me any differently. He didn't. He remained the same demanding, micromanaging person he always had been.

In fact, not only did he continue to work me hard, but he harassed me daily about when I was going to deliver. He actually said this to others who would come into our office: "Lisa is going to be like those Native Americans, the ones that had children while working in the fields. She's going to bite down on a piece of leather, have her baby, and keep on working." He also asked me constantly when my baby was going to be born, because he needed to know for his schedule. Finally, I got so tired of this that I just told him to contact the hospital commander and the two of them could arrange a date to induce my labor. Pregnancy bias existed, and policies were just not conducive to active-duty women having children while serving.

Others were absolutely wonderful to me, though. Some of the personnel assigned to the organization got together and hosted a large baby shower for me. I was relatively new and was overwhelmed by their kindness, compassion, and support. Now this was the military family that I had witnessed growing up.

As it turned out, my baby came about two weeks early. Like a good trooper I worked a full day, then went home and from there to the hospital to give birth early the next morning. I thank God that my son was born healthy, but he was very low birth weight, probably due to the stress I was under and the long hours I worked. I was only authorized four weeks of maternity leave, but I asked for more since my baby had to stay in the hospital much longer than normal. I was granted that time but was amazed yet again at how women were treated while pregnant and directly afterwards.

For the record, I must state that I was married during this time and was quite happy to be able to have a child while serving. I remember being asked by many if I was planning to stay in after giving birth. Among those asking was another general officer I had known from a previous assignment. He was sort of an informal mentor over the years. I resented that he asked me that question, as I suspect he never asked the men if they were going to remain in the service after they started families. But he was asking because he wanted to help me in getting the right jobs to match my potential, and that is exactly what he did several years later. He opened doors for me. I was being sponsored and didn't even know it. I am grateful for the first few senior officers, all white men, who saw my potential and work ethic and took a chance on me. I am sure they got hassled about it, as I did. Many would tell me that these officers were doing it only because I was a woman or a Latina. Others would be so brazen as to claim these officers were sleeping with me. They were mentoring and sponsoring me because of my talent and nothing else. I only wish they had been around at my first couple of assignments. I didn't get any real mentorship continuity until I was a very senior captain, almost a major, about ten years in, and it was by another white male. He was the best trainer I had ever had, and he became one of my mentors and sponsors. His influence on my career was huge, and I was so grateful for the network he brought me into.

After giving birth, what came as a total surprise to me was when the general I worked for and his wife were among the first to come congratulate me. This was a part of him I had never seen. He was genuinely happy, and he conveyed that to me as I lay in that hospital bed after giving birth. He was human after all. This changed my opinion of him and, as I look back, I realize that I did learn a lot from him; it just wasn't intentional mentoring on his part. I soaked up what I could and learned much about leadership. In fact, I learned a lot about how important people really are, and that to treat them with respect is much better than leading from fear.

The military is quite good at practicing realistic scenarios, so that when you face the real thing in combat you are as prepared as you can be. I certainly felt prepared when I entered the combat zone as a commander. The Air Force did an outstanding job training and preparing me for the role I would undertake. My faith prepared me as well, and I went in knowing there was a possibility of my not making it out. There is a certain amount of liberation in having that type of attitude. I wasn't scared and led boldly.

When I arrived in the Sunni Triangle of Iraq, I felt like I had stepped back in time regarding gender issues. We landed under combat operations at night, averting enemy fire as we touched down, and left the engines running as my team and I deplaned. Everyone was armed and walking around very cocky, testosterone overflowing. It didn't matter if you were an officer or enlisted, the men acted like we were back in the eighties. It was 2004, and I was the expeditionary mission support group commander. Dang the luck. For them.

LSA Anaconda or Balad AB, where we were, was the most attacked air base in Iraq. In fact, it was nicknamed "Mortarville." Combat is not for the faint of heart. It was tough going. There were not many women but there sure were lots of men, and all kinds: active duty, reserve, guard, contractors, third country nationals. I attended my first meeting there with all the commanders from all the branches as well as civilian contractors. As I walked into the meeting, all eyes went to me. I was right back at my first assignment, but this time the eye fuckery was much more advanced, much viler. This also happened at the DFAC (dining facility) or anywhere I went that wasn't around my immediate troops. I was the newest piece of meat on display. After all these years, I still stuck out.

Sexually explicit jokes, sexual banter, and racial and ethnic jokes were commonplace in combat. I felt them undressing me with their eyes and more, but this time, I was a full colonel and the equivalent of the Army's mayor for the air base. My job was to build up the base as a strategic hub for combat missions. My eagles told them to fuck off. My troops tell me that my balls were on display big-time during this deployment.

I wasn't taken seriously until the other services really needed stuff, which happened rather quickly after I arrived. Stuff like M1 Abrams tanks, fuel, food, water. You know, stuff. They quickly found out that the Air Force colonel could arrange to fly in pretty much anything. Plus, they saw how quickly we built up a tent city that had environmental control units, air conditioning and heat. We were the first on base to get running water and fixed communications, so yes, I was taken very seriously. Building up an air base is not an easy thing, and it was made that much harder by the near-constant attacks and scarcity of materials. The Marines couldn't stop thanking me for bringing twenty-one of their tanks in for the first battle of Fallujah. Combat is not pleasant; it is a tough environment. But I wasn't about to go through what I had endured in the eighties. I held my ground and led.

I brought together as many of the women in our command as I could and spoke to them quite frankly about the environment they were now in. I wanted to keep them safe, as much as I could. I told them not to be out alone, always to have a battle buddy they trusted, that they were not there to pick up men but to do a mission, and that they had no idea how long a man had been there. He might have been there a week or a year and now, in combat, all women were "tens." I told them to be watchful and careful. I had to protect them from some of the Iraqi contractors as well. Some of them thought they could be a bit touchy-feely with our women. No way would I tolerate that.

One of my young captains, my contracting officer, said the Iraqis would not speak to me because I was a woman. I was the commander, and if they wanted a contract or to work on base as a contractor, they had to get my approval. So, I told my young captain: "Tell them they don't get the job or paid until they speak with me." Money talks, even in combat. They came around.

I tire of the countless individuals who say women should not serve in combat. The reality is that the United States needs women to serve in all fields, all over the world, both in peacetime and in combat. Forget for a moment that they are qualified, that they prove every day that they can serve in harm's way, lead, and kick butt. There are simply not enough men who meet the physical, mental, legal, and medical standards. I recall being interviewed by a major newspaper on Mother's Day while in Iraq. The reporter interviewed several women and wanted to know how we felt being away from our children. I countered with, I hope you are asking this same question of the fathers who are here serving on Father's Day. I wanted to ensure that no one forgot that all of us had family back home and most of us missed them deeply.

I can only speak for myself as a woman who served in a combat environment. Think about this for a minute: I served in combat and was awarded a Bronze Star Medal for my efforts *leading in combat operations* against an enemy of the United States in 2004, when women *were not yet allowed* to serve in combat, according to military regulations. The restrictions on women serving in combat roles did not officially change until

2013, when then-Secretary of Defense Leon Panetta rescinded the prohibition. In 2015 Panetta's successor, Ashton Carter, ordered all military services to open all combat jobs to women.

But combat is not that precise, nor does it follow territorial lines. In many cases there simply are no front lines; the entire area is the combat zone. For me in Iraq in 2004, it sure felt like combat. I stopped counting after 175 rockets and mortars hit the base my troops and I were trying to build up in the middle of the Sunni Triangle. Remember, I was at "Mortarville." I could tell you if it was a 57mm rocket or an 82mm mortar simply by the whistling or whizzing sound it made as it came in. That's how up close and personal it was. We suffered casualties, as did the TCNs (third country nationals) who had been brought in by contractors to provide support. Many of them quickly departed the country when it got rough. We could not.

Early on I used to laugh at the pilots who flew in personnel and other resources, who couldn't wait to drop their cargo off, engines always running, and get the heck out of there. Attacks were commonplace and became routine to those of us who lived on the ground in that environment, building the base up so they could eventually join us once we got facilities up and hardened. We did have some of what many who were stateside would call "sick humor." Just another coping and survival mechanism.

Combat changes you. When you see such young lives destroyed by IEDs, VBIEDs, small arms, or mortar attacks, you are forever changed and cannot unsee the realities and horror of war. Many of the wounded and dead came through our air base. I will never forget standing and rendering honors to plane after plane of casualties as they were being sent home. It is so very sad to say that this became a common occurrence, but it was never common to me, as I stood there saluting, holding back tears and at times just letting them fall. Death was everywhere. You couldn't escape it, you lived and breathed it, the sights, smells, and sounds of war surrounded you. I can sometimes still hear the cries of some in the night who were so scared of dying that they slept in their body armor and helmets, or of those who had been maimed as they were being whisked away for triage. Something as simple as a barbecue with friends can bring memories of the stench of burning flesh after an attack. Everyday sounds can take me right back to the Sunni Triangle. A car backfiring might sound like incoming fire.

It was early in the war with Iraq, and we were not supposed to fly the American flag. I made the decision to allow a memorial to be erected and a flag to be flown at half-mast at the site of our fallen. It was crude, but effective. I wanted to provide a way for the troops to mourn. For twenty-four hours I let the memorial site stay up, then I told the troops to take it down and erect another tent in the same place and put some troops in it; we had to move on and concentrate on the mission at hand. I realized that some considered my actions cold and callous, but I had a job to do. I also knew that combat doesn't really allow you to properly mourn. That comes later, sometimes much later, when you least expect or want. I only hoped that when they really did mourn they would be surrounded by people who got it, who understood the depth of the loss they experienced.

I never wanted to kill the enemy as much as I did after our first casualties. It was frightening to me just how intense my feelings were at the time. I look back now and can't believe just how deeply ingrained it was in me to kill the enemy. You don't deal with these feelings at the time. It isn't the place, and you don't have the time; you are focused on the mission. I must admit that even today, years later, I am still shocked at my own intense feelings of wanting to kill an enemy.

Until the moment I landed in Iraq, all throughout the advance preparations, practicing over and over again how to set up a bare base, fortify tents, put in comms, simulate convoy runs with opposing forces, and all the frenzy that comes with prepping to go into harm's way, a part of me was thinking I would be called back at some point before I landed. After all I had been through just to get to the level I now was at, that little voice in the back of my head was telling me that they really didn't want to send a woman into that part of the world as a commander. It was 2004 and women had come a long way already, but I still thought this.

During attacks and when we went outside the wire, we all took evasive action and hunkered down when we could. There was no distinguishing between men and women; we were all on the same side and had each other's back. No one said to me, "You aren't supposed to be here." Hell, they wanted and needed me there. I had the requisite leadership experience and the expertise in expeditionary combat support. I was a *by name request* to serve as a commander in Iraq by the Chief of Staff of the Air Force.

My leadership experiences as a commander in combat are for another book, but I'll talk here about something that no one really talks about regarding women in combat: feminine hygiene.

Some women take shots to keep from having periods while deployed. Others do not. It is an individual choice made by all women. I spoke with my doctor about it and since I was older, he suggested that I not get the shots. He and other physicians were concerned that the shots might induce early menopause as a side effect. And no one thought having a commander in Iraq with menopausal symptoms was a good idea. I certainly didn't and wasn't about to leave anything to chance. I wanted to be prepared. Just the fact that I had to have these conversations with several male physicians was an issue for me, but there was no way you were keeping me out of the fight.

So, I was offered female hormone pills to keep from having a period. I started taking them before I deployed to ensure they worked. They did. I was to take one a day. I would probably never have taken this hormone if I wasn't being deployed in combat, but I thought it was the best-case scenario, and there was no way I wasn't going to go.

Remember that by name request? Imagine how much I might have set back women serving if I had said I could not go because of my GYN issues. I did not discuss this level of detail or these thoughts with anyone. This was a personal choice for me, and I chose to go. As a commander, I could not ask my troops to do something that I would not do. I felt very strongly about serving in combat alongside my troops. Besides, I *was* the right *person* for this job.

I had been in country only a short time when I noticed that the porta potties were an issue. Have you ever followed a six-foot-three-inch guy after he has used the porta potty? Not pleasant under any circumstances, never mind in extreme heat and during attacks. Not only is the smell bad, but typically there's no toilet tissue or hand sanitizer left. I noticed that some of the women were having their periods, and there was no privacy for them when using a porty potty. The men who followed would notice that you were on your period. We had enough to deal with; women didn't need that particular kind of hazing.

I labeled several porta potties as women only, and immediately there no longer were issues with lack of toilet tissue or hand sanitizer. They were the best kept porta potties on the base! All of them had signs inside and out saying that any unauthorized use would be dealt with, by me, the Expeditionary Mission Support Group Commander (EMSG/CC).

I had picked one that was the closest to our headquarters facility and labeled it women only, and I had a wonderful time observing someone tell the male general, my boss, that he was no longer authorized to use it. I am not stupid. I had picked that one because it was close to the headquarters where I worked and was the only one on base that had been wired with lights. My boss was not excited that I had done this, especially when he was caught using it.

I relocated the smoking pits, where troops would gather to smoke and hang, as they had been placed right in front of the latrines and showers. It became obvious to me that this position allowed many men to literally watch us women go to the latrines, probably even notice a pattern of our usage. I didn't want to provide another opportunity for enhanced hazing. People bitched and moaned about it, but being the commander, I used my eagles to make sure all our people were valued, not just some. I respected the women who served and took actions needed to ensure that not only did I hear them, but I saw them and appreciated their efforts and did everything I could to keep them safe. I wonder if a male commander back then would have thought about these particular issues.

What took me somewhat by surprise was the response from women. I knew my decisions would have an impact, but I totally underestimated it. Women started coming up to me and thanking me for designating several porta potties women only, praising my leadership in including them. It made a huge difference for the women's morale. It is a tough environment and then to have to deal with crappy, pardon the pun, porta potties and hazing because you're on your period – I had to do something about it, and I did. Little did I know that I would soon come to appreciate this action myself.

The pills I was taking worked for about a month in country, then they just stopped working. I couldn't stop bleeding. And this was not spotty bleeding, but very heavy, clotting bleeding. We were using porta potties, communal showers, lots of sand, grit and grime, not the best place for this to come up. Initially I told only my executive officer, someone I trusted with my life. I had no pads or tampons. I wasn't supposed to bleed. He found me some. He was over six feet tall and probably got some looks when he did that. Maybe he told anyone who asked that they were for wound management; before joining the Air Force he had been a medic in the Army.

The only other soul I told was our med tech, who was a TSgt (E-6). She tried calling late at night to reach a military medical center in the States, to get advice on what to do. It was too early in our base buildup for us to have a full-fledged hospital set up. So we were on our own to figure this one out with what we had on hand. We worked it out. I had to substantially increase the number of hormone pills I took daily. It took a while, but the bleeding eventually stopped.

It never entered my mind to trust anyone above me with this. The only person who outranked me was the general, and I just didn't feel comfortable reporting my medical situation to him or anyone back at CENTCOM in Florida. I tried to keep it all under wraps and stay focused on the mission. It was a tough mission, with near-daily attacks. This was just another challenge for me to face head on and deal with. I was afraid to be sent home and worked very hard not to let anyone know what was going on.

It felt like being right back in that fighter squadron when I first came in the service: the same feelings of isolation, fear of retaliation, fear of being thought of as not hacking it as a woman, as a Latina. I had to prove women could serve in combat and still do the job, even when dealing with intense stressors on our bodies. You would have to scrape me off the ground before I would physically give up.

So once again I suffered in silence, sucked up the pain, dealt with the blood loss as best I could, and pressed on to do my job. Nobody but the two I mentioned ever knew. On the way home, I asked several of my senior commanders and senior enlisted if they had thought something was off with me during the deployment. None had; they all said what a great job I had done under extreme adversity and duress. They were talking about the austere conditions, attacks, limited resources, and casualties. They had no idea how much adversity I personally had been under. I had mastered the skills of compartmentalization and embracing the suck better than I had thought.

What did this situation really do to my body? Who really knows the extent of it all, but I did have to have a hysterectomy within two weeks of coming home. First time in years that I had taken time off, and it was for that. So, after my surgery I worked half days from home and tried to let my body heal. It's hard when you want to be with your troops, and at the same time you want to be home with your family. I found it even harder after Iraq, because those troops were my family now. Would I do it again, the same way? Damn straight I would.

The military is tough no matter who you are. Then to have to fend off predators from within as you train in preparation for going up against an enemy, and then to go up against that external enemy, only to find that sometimes the enemy is the one right next to you. This is the deepest form of betrayal to experience from a brother you trusted with your life. So, yes, I am angry at what happened to me in those early years and what continues to happen to others.

But at the same time, I experienced great friendships and bonds with some of the men and women who served with me. We overcame huge obstacles to achieve our mission. These are the true professionals who had my back, and I had theirs. There probably isn't anything I wouldn't do for them, especially those I served with in combat. That sort of bond is forever unbreakable. I keep in touch with many I served with. For every vile predator in the military, there are thousands of outstanding troops who represent everything that is right about our country.

For me, the military brings both outstanding and horrific memories. I learned so much, traveled all over the world, have friendships that continue to this day, grew into an outstanding leader, and helped as many as I could.

The military gave me so much opportunity in training, education, and leadership. It was up to me what I did with that opportunity. But they also put me in harm's way, not only in combat but in initial training and those first assignments. Those first years, the assault and ongoing harassment affected me more than I ever knew. I was so good at compartmentalization, normalizing bad behavior, that for many years I either forgot or just chalked it up as just the way it was. I have chronic pain and medical conditions directly tied to my assault, harassment, and service. There are so many like me, who suffered in silence or spoke out and were retaliated against and never received the justice or support they deserved.

I started out as someone just trying to survive, then someone working hard to prove myself by my actions, achievements that served as evidence that women not only belong but can be outstanding leaders. I proved it all. But at what cost? Not only to me and my family, but to countless others who are still being sexually harassed and assaulted in the military. I speak up now and tell my story for them, and to make up for all the lost time in not having done so. Don't get me wrong; I know full well that if I had brought up my assault and harassment at OTS, I would have been kicked out, and if I had said something during those first few assignments, I would not have progressed up the ranks or gotten the select assignments, command billets, and schooling needed for advancement.

Every one of my accomplishments was earned; nothing was handed to me or easy. I heard countless times, for each of my promotions or achievements, that it was only because I was a woman or a Latina. No, it was because I worked my butt off and someone actually paid attention enough to recognize it, or I brought it to their attention. I sometimes think: What if I had never been assaulted or harassed? Would I have been an even better leader? Would I have progressed further? Having to fight for your very survival early on in the military, then fight for equity, and still be able to achieve the level of success I have, tells me that I was indeed held back by a system, an infrastructure that has refused to change to truly welcome women and allow them to flourish. Two of the biggest reasons we've never had critical mass with women serving are the toxic climate and policies that are not conducive. The military says they want women, yet their very policies are not inclusive in so many ways. When I entered the military all those years ago, I was issued some clothing and uniform items that were made for men. They had not been tailored or made for women, and that includes some of the gear we used. The crotch on my fatigues was so long and cumbersome – what was I supposed to do with that? Even in Iraq I wore men's combat body armor. Why? Because no women's body armor existed. It has only been in the last few years that it is being developed.

Now that I am on my healing journey, remembering, reflecting on, and acknowledging what happened to me, I understand that I was not at fault. I wasn't the predator, and I am much more than a survivor of MST. Recently, while undergoing a form of therapy with the VA called EMDR (Eye Movement Desensitization and Reprocessing), I came to the realization that what I thought were fragments of one assault at OTS were in fact memories of multiple events. Picking up the pieces, the fractions of my past, is a tough road to be on, but I know that this is where the Lord has led me. I am finally on the path I was destined to be on, authentically helping to heal not only myself but others as well. Going through this therapy, writing, and speaking with others who have experienced MST or combat experiences have been cathartic in many ways. I now feel that with every word I write, every poem I pen, I am slowly taking back my past, owning it, and allowing that slow death of a thousand cuts that I underwent of sexual assault, sexual harassment, and more to finally begin to heal, one cut, one word at a time.

I can stand here today and tell you that I chose to stay in and prove my competence, baffle them with my excellence, so they couldn't say the "women experiment" didn't work. I now can speak up with a track record of proven performance, both in peacetime and in combat. They cannot take that away from me. I know I made a difference serving and leading. But there is a little voice in the back of my head that rears up, asking, "What if you had spoken up back then? What if it had made a difference?" Would it have saved countless others from sexual assault and harassment? That keeps me up at night. *No más!* No more must suffer because an institution refuses to transform itself and its culture.

CHAPTER 2

THE GRUNT

Sue Caldwell

Immediately upon my arrival in Vietnam, I heard my fellow soldiers say, "Look, guys, the Army sent us a whore!"

And that's how Sue Caldwell was greeted when she stepped onto the tarmac in Bien Hoa, Vietnam in 1969, as a new Army recruit at 19. She joined the Women's Army Corps (WAC) upon completion of high school and immediately found herself right smack in the middle of a war. Sue *volunteered to serve* as a grunt in Vietnam as she was escaping a homelife rife with years of both physical and verbal abuse. So she went from one type of war at home right into another one, but this one had very real bullets and mortars coming in. It wasn't the first time or the last time that she would be in harm's way.

Despite all the denigration, sexual taunts, harassment, and attempted assaults, Sue liked serving her country and excelled. "I have never regretted going to Vietnam despite having horrible experiences there," she says. "I'm always proud of my service." The combined traumas that she experienced while growing up, in the military, and in civilian life were seemingly more than any one person could have withstood. But she endured, surviving each time when she should have died. She gets knocked down and gets back up, staying in the ring and ultimately kicking life's ass, rising like a phoenix. Sue powerfully exudes an indomitable spirit.

Sue grew up in Texas in abject poverty. Indoor plumbing was a luxury her family didn't have, and there were times when food was barely enough for the family of four. Sue's family didn't show affection. Her mother never hugged her, smiled at her, gave her gifts, or even acknowledged her. There simply were no affirmations of the kind children normally receive from their mothers. Her mother had also grown up in abuse and continued the cycle with her own family.

Sue's mother was known throughout their rural town as an abusive, bitter, and cruel woman. Some locals even tried to intervene in their own way, such as by keeping Sue in school beyond the release time, attempting to minimize the abuse they almost certainly knew she experienced at home. This was the 1950s, and families were freer to raise their children as they saw fit, even if that included physical and emotional abuse. Sue says that you basically were "owned" by your parents, and that she was her parents' property to do with as they wished.

Sue's mother beat her daily and abused her emotionally, making her feel inconsequential, lower than nothing. Sue was routinely yelled at, slapped, thrown about, even attacked on occasion with a knife or gun. Once Sue started to mature as a young woman, her mother threatened to cut off her breasts and mutilate her genitals. All the beatings occurred when Sue was alone with her mother, never when her father was present. After one horrific attack with a gun, Sue's father took her out of the home to live with other relatives, trying to keep her safe. That turned out to be temporary; she was brought right back to the same abusive, toxic, and emotionally barren household.

This day in, day out abuse lasted for eighteen years, until Sue got the heck out of there. Her mother was a narcissist and wanted all attention on herself. If people paid any attention to Sue or her father, they both had hell to pay. So her father stopped paying attention to Sue to save her from her mother. One time her father made Sue a rudimentary doll-like figure. She treasured it and kept it hidden from her mother. That was one of the only gifts she ever received from her family.

Sue had a secret that many people didn't know: She was really, really smart. And she had hope and that indomitable spirit. She was, and still is, much more than a survivor. She grew up speaking German, but quickly picked up English in elementary school even faster and better than her older brother, which also caused her to be on the receiving end of some unfortunate mistreatment.

It is almost impossible to imagine what Sue went through, but despite it all she excelled in school and was very active in every aspect of her education, including extracurricular activities like sports and writing for the school newspaper. She became the first in her family to progress beyond the sixth grade, and the only one to go on to college and obtain multiple degrees, including a PhD.

After graduating high school at seventeen, Sue pulled cotton. This was something she had done every summer since she was twelve. A local banker told her she should leave town and not look back, that he saw potential in her. He was a former military man, and he encouraged her to get away. She considered both the Peace Corps and the military, but the Peace Corps didn't have the GI Bill. So at eighteen Sue decided to join the military. The recruiter said he had to speak to her parents; he wanted their signed permission. Her mother cussed her out and threw things at her, but ultimately both her parents signed.

Sue couldn't wait to leave home. She was running as far as she could from the black hole of her home life. She was getting out! "The service became my window to the world, gave me a way out, and finally allowed me to see a future," she told me. She went to boot camp in Alabama and ended up at the Pentagon for her first assignment. Washington, DC was the furthest she could think of at the time that she could be. Ironically, it was from there that she volunteered for Vietnam, which was truly the farthest away from her mother that she could possibly go.

So in 1967 Sue joined the Women's Army Corps (WAC).[1] These women soldiers were referred to as WACs. Basically she was a grunt, an enlisted troop working as a clerk/typist and in personnel management.

---

1 See "History of the WAC and Army Women," https://www.armywomen.org/wacHistory.shtml.

45

It is important to put Sue's service era into context. What exactly was the Women's Army Corps? It was the women's branch of the Army, which began in 1941 as the Women's Army Auxiliary Corps (WAAC), was approved by Congress in 1942, then evolved into active-duty status with the creation of the WAC in 1943. Following the active-duty status of the WAC, the WAAC was discontinued. The WAC was disestablished by Congress in 1978, as women were being assimilated into the main structure of the Army.

Fort McClellan, Alabama was the location for both boot camp and advanced individual training (AIT) for Sue. She graduated from both at the top of her class and was given first choice of assignment. The trainees and drill instructors there were all women. It wasn't until she arrived at the Pentagon that she finally worked around men.

At the Pentagon, Sue was an E-2. You couldn't get much lower ranked than that. Field grade and senior officers were rampant throughout the Pentagon, especially in the office she ended up at, the Vice Chief of Staff for Logistics for the Army. Her work was outstanding and she made rank quickly, promoted to E-5 in her first year of service, drawing comments like "She's on the fast track, must have slept with someone."

She experienced the typical sexism and misogyny that many took to be just the way it was. Her boss, a colonel, called her "his girl" and made comments like, "I'll get my girl to do that." Sue noticed that he didn't speak that way about the men. The colonel even wanted to meet and interview all the men she dated. "This was the late sixties," she says. "Women were like property. It was like the colonel calling me his girl, his little girl. That always grated on me, but he was quite the mentor." It was sort of strange how he tried to look out for her and at the same time denigrate her, and didn't think twice about it.

An incident she recalls while working at the Pentagon involved her staying late one night, as she often did, typing papers for all the guys in the office who were working on their master's degrees. Typing their personal schoolwork was not in her job description, but she did it anyway. She sort of felt she needed to. One night one of the guys, a Department of the Army civil service staff member (GS-13), stayed late and, after she finished typing his paper, offered to take her to get something to eat and give her a ride home.

Everything was fine at first. They got something to eat, but on the way to the barracks she noticed he was going the wrong way. He kept telling her, "I just want to get to know you better." He drove to a park near the Potomac River and proceeded to take her hand and place it on his groin. He wanted to know her in a way she wanted no part of. Sue jumped out of the vehicle, ran straight into the river in her uniform, swam out about fifty feet, and started treading water. He started walking toward her in the river. She was terrified that he was going to rape her.

Finally, after he repeatedly said he wouldn't hurt her and would take her home, she got out of the water, still dripping wet. She was freezing, her teeth chattered, she couldn't stop shaking. But she had to get out of there, so she finally relented and sat in the back seat of the car, and he drove her to her barracks. She arrived in her room sometime after midnight.

She recalls an incident involving a lieutenant colonel who would come on to her making sexist comments and innuendos. Since he was so high ranking, she didn't believe she could say anything back to him. There was no one to report this type of behavior to. "If I reported anything at all, I would have been kicked out of the Army," she told me. "I was told that it comes with the territory. So I learned, like others, to suffer in silence."

Word got around while she was working at the Pentagon that she wasn't going to put out and they begin to call her NATO, which stood for "no action, talk only." Sue was very happy being referred to as NATO. It beat the alternative, which was being called a whore. Another time she was told that WACs were good for screwing, not marrying. The overt sexism was everywhere.

Every incident of military sexual trauma (MST) that Sue experienced was perpetrated by older men, never by junior or young ones. These men all had power over her. Sue remarks that it was almost like a sport to them, a conquest, as if women were there to serve them, as if it was just expected. "When I raised my right hand to serve my country, little did I know that I was to serve my male comrades," says Sue.

She volunteered for Vietnam and the colonel tried to talk her out of it, but Sue wouldn't have it. She had joined the Army to be a soldier. She wasn't pretending; she had trained to go to war and felt ready to do that. She remembers someone from her hometown who had gone to Vietnam and come back totally different. But she was curious and idealistic, and her mind was made up: She was going.

Sue was nineteen years old, good-looking, blonde, had been in the Army only two years, and was a volunteer. She stood out, whether she wanted to or not. It was 1969, and women made up barely one percent of the active duty force. Sue recalls that when she was in Vietnam, there were usually about eighty or ninety WACs on the ground, and about fifty thousand guys.

You can do the math. This was the very definition of a man's world, made even worse by the reality that the bulk of them were draftees who didn't want to serve and certainly didn't want to be in Vietnam. "Immediately upon my arrival in Vietnam," she told me, "I heard my fellow soldiers say, 'Look, guys, the Army sent us a whore!'" That first week alone, there were many bets among the men as to who would sleep with her first. No one won those bets.

According to the Veterans of Foreign Wars (VFW), the United States had over 250,000 women serving during the Vietnam War. But only about 7,500 served in the war zone. Many were stationed throughout the Pacific or at hospitals in the States. Approximately 85 percent of women who served in country in Vietnam were nurses in the Army, Navy, or Air Force. The other 15 percent, like Sue, were not, and their stories are few and far between. Their roles were medical service corps, air traffic controllers, communications specialists, intelligence officers, clerks, personnel management, and Red Cross volunteers (Donut Dollies).[2]

It was extremely tough duty with no frontlines. Small arms fire, rockets, and mortars were commonplace. Sue was not a nurse. She was literally a grunt, like many of the men who served in Vietnam. But when she tells people she served in Vietnam, they automatically assume she was a nurse. The story of the WACs and their contributions are an important part of American history, but not commonly known.

---

2 "VFW Salutes Women Veterans," *VFW Magazine*, March 2021, p. 2.

Sue was smart and cocky and entered the war zone already believing that she wouldn't make it home alive. That afforded her the freedom to do her job, as she had no inhibitions or fear of dying. She continued to make rank fast, was promoted to E-6, and was known as someone who got shit done. "I earned the respect of the comrades in my unit, and they kept my back like I kept theirs," she recalls. "There were many others, however, who considered abusing me as a sport."

Within a week of arriving, she became the noncommissioned officer in charge (NCOIC) of a small team of men. This was interesting, as typically WACs were allowed to supervise only other WACs, not men in the regular Army. She really wasn't considered a leader unless she led other WACs.

So in reality here she is, overseeing men, an NCOIC, a leader without a weapon. No weapons were issued to the WACs. All the men were armed, but the women were not. She was a leader in charge of men but, because she was a woman, she wasn't allowed to be issued a weapon. Her authority had been undermined from day one.

How was she going to protect herself if the area got overrun? Sue had a plan for that: She and the other WACs were going to overpower the sentry, a male Army E-3, who stood outside the detachment to protect them from both their brothers in arms and the Vietcong. How were they going to do that? One of them was going to flirt with him, Sue was going to kick him in the balls, and another was going to grab his gun. Imagine having to come up with a plan like this because you were not allowed to have a weapon in the middle of a war zone.

Sue's nickname in Vietnam was Half Pint, probably due to her short stature and how cocky she was. But she was well respected, performed her job well, and had positional power, as she was the one who had come from the Pentagon and reassigned officers from across the Army, in and out of Vietnam. They even sometimes called her Headquarters, as she was in daily contact with the Pentagon. Sue always focused on the mission and never considered her own feelings. "The Army didn't issue feelings or opinions, so I didn't have any," she says. "No matter what happened, I didn't cry."

Half Pint was not given the same rank as the men who had similar duties, such as the sergeant in charge of reassigning enlisted. He had a higher rank than she did, even though she was in charge of reassigning officers. She had what we now call social capital; she had informal power, and that helped her somewhat during her year in country.

Everyday life was extremely difficult. Drinking and drugs were quite common and everywhere in Vietnam. Sue recalls drinking heavily on many occasions, especially while hunkered down in bunkers during attacks. They even had canteens labeled Bourbon, Scotch, Vodka. She smoked; everyone did. She was on the receiving end of relentless harassment and was constantly ogled. Vietnamese men tried to just touch her, as she was one of the few female "round eyes" around. She was always on guard, one eye focused on keeping her fellow soldiers at bay, the other on point for the enemy, who was everywhere. One of Sue's very real concerns was friendly fire.

On one occasion during a mortar attack, Half Pint found herself on the opposite end of the base from the WAC bunker. She had been out exercising and needed to run to that bunker to withstand the attack, but it was simply too far. Mortars were landing all around her as she ran. She ran into the nearest bunker loaded with sandbags, which turned out to be an MP station. She slammed into the bunker and was met with the hard stares of fifteen men.

Drugs and alcohol were everywhere, and all eyes were on her. Several of the men were half clothed and drunk or high, and when they saw this young, blonde thing, they went for her. She felt arms all over her body; she screamed for them to get away from her. She tried to fight them off, kicking, screaming, striking out. She was knocked to the floor. One grabbed her arm, another put his hand on her mouth to stop her from screaming. Half Pint bit the crap out of that hand; he let go, giving her enough time to wrestle loose from the others and get out of there. She ran from the safety of a hardened bunker, but away from the looming assault and rape, right back into the open where mortars were still raining down. She took her chances with the mortars. That, to her, was safer than staying with those MPs.

Half Pint is not sure how she made it back to the WAC bunker, but she was running for her life. She had been a track star in high school, only two years prior. She ran on instinct and prior training. In the WAC bunker, in the pitch black inside, she finally allowed herself to breathe. She was shaking, whimpering, couldn't speak or answer anyone, stayed lying on the ground, shivered for hours as the mortar attack lasted through the night. "No one asked me what had happened, why it took me so long to get to the bunker," she says.

She can still remember the cold fear in her gut as she lay on the floor in that MP hooch, with the faces, arms, and bodies of all the men closing in on her. It's not a surprise that she has trust issues with MPs or cops. They are supposed to protect and defend, not attack you, not attempt a gang rape in a war zone. The nightmares have not gone away, and they come back with a vengeance when least expected. Can any of us ever really forget the traumas we experience?

Another disturbing experience occurred with someone she trusted with her life, one of her superior officers. They literally had been through hell together in Vietnam, so the deep betrayal she experienced when he sexually assaulted her still burns brightly in her mind and haunts her.

They were on the far end of the base. Half Pint had to make radio calls back to the Pentagon, and these were usually done in the middle of the night due to the time difference. Someone would always stay behind and give her a ride back to the WAC detachment area. On the way back one night, this officer said he wanted to show her his hooch. She didn't think anything of this, as they had worked together for months and he was more than a fellow soldier: He was her brother, her confidant.

Entering his hooch, she saw a photograph of his wife. He moved to it and turned it down so she couldn't see it. Or perhaps he did it so his wife couldn't see what he had planned next. He told Sue to lie on his cot, then he got on top of her and immediately ejaculated. At that very second, before she could even process what had just happened, the sirens went off and they were under attack. They ran to a bunker. He mumbled something to a colonel about why she was there, as normally she would be in the WAC bunker. Half Pint just sat in silence, too stunned to talk.

She recalls this incident with shame and pain. She can still feel the warmth of his ejaculation through her fatigues. "Fifty-two years ago, and I can't get myself to get through it," she says. "All the others I can somehow process, but not this one. Of all the guys there, I trusted him unequivocally, never a doubt, never a question, and then he betrays me."

Six weeks before she left Vietnam, there was a major mortar attack and Half Pint was knocked down and injured her back. She was in the hospital for nine days and was told by a doctor that she also had shell shock. The doctor offered to send her back to the States, but she said no and went back to her unit to finish out her tour.

Leaving Vietnam is ingrained in her mind. She was on a commercial contract flight that landed in Oakland, California late at night due to all the protestors that typically surrounded most things having to do with the Vietnam War. It was a dark period in American history. She remembers landing, then being asked if she wanted a quick exit from the Army or the standard physical and administrative actions. Sue stated quite strongly: "I am getting out of this man's Army." She chose the getting out by sunup option. Discharge papers were being processed right there at the airport. When she got to her turn in line, a lieutenant started harassing her about not being in proper uniform and her hair being too long. Sue and her fellow soldiers had just flown halfway around the world, had seen action just hours before they left, and were not in the mood for this type of bureaucratic BS. Many had post-traumatic stress, but back then they were told they had shell shock. They had no patience for how the separations were being conducted. In fact, several other enlisted soldiers grabbed the lieutenant by his throat and informed him that he would sign her separation papers, now! And he did.

People on the plane she took back to Texas just stared at her, as if she were some sort of creature from outer space. They parted for her to walk past; no one wanted to be near her. She probably had that thousand-yard stare that is often associated with combat veterans. It was almost as if she were contaminated. Not one person spoke to her. She had just fought for her country and returned to an ungrateful nation. She was twenty years old and had already lived a lifetime.

Her family greeted her late at night. Her father actually put his arm on her shoulder and said that she looked sick. Her mother was bitching about how long they had to wait for her. One of her aunts remarked that Sue had gotten the Bronze Star, as her father had before her. Her father just stared at her, not a word between them. But for the first time in her life, Sue felt a bond pass between them. It took the similar experiences of two different wars for them to feel something for each other, even if it was only respect. Her father had served in World War II and had been a POW, but never spoke of his experience.

The months and years following her return are still filled with symptoms of PTSD, issues with reintegration into civilian life, and coming to terms with her combat service. She saw various therapists. Some helped more than others. She became well enough to move forward, earning several degrees, including a PhD, and got married. She became quite successful in her endeavors. But she never really spoke about the realities of her wartime experiences or her MST.

At age twenty, she discovered she had breast cancer. Could this have been due to exposure to Agent Orange? She remembers filling out paperwork for Agent Orange screening post-Vietnam. The forms said she had to provide a semen sample and, incredibly, she was told by a nurse that her paperwork could not be completed and processed until one was provided. After experiencing so much MST while serving, and then to hear that? The VA forms had been created for men, not women, just like most of what she experienced in the military, from the way her uniforms didn't fit to how weapons were issued.

In 1972, Sue had what is called a psychotic episode and was hospitalized. She was drugged quite heavily for some time. Her therapist and an associate became instrumental in her healing journey. Even back then she didn't speak about all her trauma. That didn't occur until 1995, when she was finally able to describe several of the traumas that she had experienced as a young girl and in the military. But she still didn't speak about the MST. That didn't happen until many years later. In fact, Sue says that I am the first person to hear the full accounting of her MST experiences. She told me:

> What I have realized is that what happened in my childhood has marked me for life. It set so many things into motion. For many decades, I have been so guarded about my inner self, making sure

I stay protected. I need to take care of that little girl; she has been hurt enough.

And just when you might have thought that was the end of her traumatic experiences, in 1995 Sue was hit by a drunk driver, leaving her near death. She suffered 45 fractures, a traumatic brain injury, and a punctured lung, lost several organs, and was not expected to live. But here came that indomitable spirit that she has. After two years in five different hospitals, countless surgeries, and years of physical therapy, she was back among the living, albeit with residual medical issues. That warrior spirit continues contributing to society and touching many lives – mine included.

Serving as a leader within the VFW, Sue served as a both a district commander and a post commander, then became a statewide leader. She became the first woman state inspector and the first woman state judge advocate in Texas. This was important as more and more women role models were needed throughout the VFW and still are. But not even this service was without sexual trauma. She was sexually assaulted at a national VFW convention, reported it, and was defended by her fellow VFW leaders. In her case, the VFW leaders took all the right actions.

Sue taught at the community college level, started educational services for military personnel overseas, and worked various other jobs, never letting anyone put her in a box and define who she is. She learned to stand up for herself after a life filled with tragic experiences. She says: "Bad things happen, shit happens to you, whether you are rich, poor, disadvantaged. The important thing is not to allow the crisis or event to define you."

Sue's journey has been a long and difficult one, never easy. She never realized just how much she had internalized, how much of her trauma she had buried, until she sat down with me for interviews for this book. Much of what is in this recounting has never before been publicly shared. Even though Sue buried some of what happened to her, her mind and body never forgot; they continued to keep track of all her lived experiences and traumas. I find myself wanting to take the pain away for her, lessen it somehow. But all I can do is listen, honor her lived experiences, and share her story, in hopes others will understand that they are not alone, that military sexual trauma lingers, ripping through and littering the lives it has touched. Sue's story and the many that follow demand that the military culture must change.

I've encouraged Half Pint to write about her experiences, and she is doing just that. I hope it helps her continued healing. We speak often about our trauma and our healing journeys.

CHAPTER 3

THE SHIRT

Audrey Magnuson

Although I was sexually harassed and pursued by predators, the system worked for me in the two instances that I experienced. My chain of command responded with speed, appropriateness, and intolerance towards what occurred.

Audrey Magnuson enlisted into the service at 18 years old and found herself at a small base overseas after basic and initial training. The base was not what some would call a good fit for a slick sleeve's first assignment, as it was often considered a remote and isolated tour with limited support. Little did Audrey know just how isolated she would become at that first duty assignment so far away from the world back home.

Yet she would also come to learn about how the military can circle its wagons to defend its own. How military personnel can at times act like a true family and be there for each other, rescuing her from repeated sexual trauma. On the one hand, she experienced this harrowing behavior, yet others stepped in to create a protective cocoon around her. She encountered both predators and protectors.

I first met Audrey around 2010, when I retired from active-duty service and began a second career in higher education. She was the career center director at The University of Texas at San Antonio, and I was a newly appointed associate provost. I reached out to various leaders across the campus to gain a pulse of the institution, see where the landmines were, and learn how I could assist others.

Audrey was one of the first people I reached out to, as I heard that she had served in the military. There ended up being more than a fleeting military connection, and she became a confidante and friend, as well as a colleague.

Instantly upon meeting Audrey, I felt an immediate kinship. She reminded me of what was the best thing about the military: its people. She carried herself like the professional leader that she was, full of confidence and knowledge and always willing to help others succeed, especially our students. She was totally put together, had truly made the transition to the civilian workplace very well. I was impressed with that. She had been successful in the military and was succeeding in higher ed, exactly as I hoped to do.

In the military, Audrey had risen to the rank of E-8, a Senior Master Sergeant in the Air Force. Not an easy task for anyone, especially not for a woman who came into the service in 1980. Not only did she achieve the second highest enlisted rank, but she became a First Sergeant, or what we affectionately call a Shirt. Her lived experiences helped shape the way that she embraced her role as a Shirt. The Shirt is an indispensable right hand to the Commander. For you *Game of Thrones* fans, Audrey served in the role of The Hand, as a coach, a mentor, a disciplinarian, and more. Her job was people, as she is fond of saying. She took her role seriously and helped many.

Why did Audrey decide to join the military? What made her want to serve and put others first? Within five minutes of meeting her, you will understand that she is a giver, one that helps others and their needs first. That selfless trait couldn't have lined up more perfectly with the core values of the Air Force.

Audrey was born in San Antonio and raised in Austin, and brought up as a Catholic. Both her parents were born and raised in San Antonio. However, they were living in California due to her father being a PhD. candidate at UC-Berkeley when Audrey was expected to be born. Her mother returned to Texas to have her. There was no way she would have her daughter be born in California. That Texas pride ran deep.

Her father ended up at UT-Austin as a professor, and that is where Audrey grew up, the middle child. She had three siblings: an older sister and brother and a younger sister. They lived in an affluent neighborhood, and Audrey attended LC Anderson High School. After she graduated, her family moved to San Antonio as her father began working in private industry. Audrey's whole world changed. Moving turned her life upside down and really upset her social structure. She says it totally upset her apple cart. She had a high school sweetheart that she was serious with. As much as a 17-year-old can be serious that is.

Audrey wasn't sure what to do with her life after graduation. All she knew was that she wanted to help others, so she applied and was accepted to nursing school. She didn't get a lot of mentoring from her father on life after high school; she was on her own trying to figure it all out, and it was almost like being first generation to attend college, as there was a complete absence of any guidance. Perhaps that was what her father intended: to let her learn on her own the ways of the world. However, a little guidance would have been helpful as her father had navigated higher ed pursing his PhD, worked in academia, and had years of experience.

The frustrations mounted for Audrey: what to do? She decided to just get the hell out of Dodge, didn't ask anyone's permission, went to see military recruiters. She knew she wanted out and wanted to do some traveling. She was sort of running away from her life, from her family and wanted to see the world, to do something brave and unusual. Indeed, she harbored a secret: She had always wanted to join the military, but never shared that dream. Her father was very authoritative and judgmental, had been at Berkeley, and had a negative impression of the military.

Audrey saw the military completely differently, as an honorable profession. Deep down she just knew that the military would provide her the opportunity to help people while experiencing something exciting and different. She spoke with the Army and the Air Force and ended up going Air Force because it gave her the best opportunity to go into the medical profession.

Her father was furious. Her mother never really said what she thought. Her father told her, "You are not going to ever succeed at this." Audrey thought to herself, "Just watch this." She had disappointed her father, and he let her know it. A determined eighteen-year-old with something to prove left for basic training within 24 hours of signing up. From being an Honor Grad at basic training, to obtaining both bachelor's and master's degrees, to her successful military career of more than twenty years, Audrey had the last word. Her performance speaks for itself.

Her high school sweetheart followed her into the service and she married him, but it ended up being a short marriage, only eighteen months. He cheated on her, and she could not let that stand. But the whole marriage situation, that broken trust and her vulnerability, just complicated things. It allowed a predator to sneak in and use all of that against Audrey during her very first assignment overseas.

I recall an occasion several years ago when my department at The University of Texas at San Antonio conducted a series of events throughout the week commemorating Veterans Day. This particular event, specifically designed for women veterans, was a luncheon where several women vets were speaking about their military service, and the subject turned to harassment. The women had served in different branches and were different ranks, and several had combat experience. It started out as a panel and ended up a free-for-all discussion. All women present said they had experienced some form of sexual harassment or sexism, me included. All except for Audrey.

Audrey said that she had not experienced anything like what the rest of us did. We chalked it up to the fact that she had been a medical technician in the military and had flown medevac, and that the medical field was indeed different from the rest.

I remember being incredulous. She had joined the military just one month after I had, and I remember all too well what it was like back then. I recall saying to her, "Wow, what Air Force were you in? Certainly not the one I was in."

As I reflect on this, I am so sorry for how I responded to her. I now know how difficult it is for anyone to speak up, and I should not have pressed her the way I and others did. Perhaps she didn't even recollect exactly what had transpired, or was just not ready to share in a group setting. Through my own experience, I have learned that each of us must come to our own decision as to whether and when we speak up, and in what manner.

Some may be like me and buried it so deeply that it was long forgotten. Others will decide never to speak of their MST experiences. Some may speak up openly. It is an individual choice, and it is not up to us to judge or press. At that event, none of us had any idea just how deeply what had happened to her at her first assignment had stayed with her.

It was years into our friendship before I became aware of what had transpired. It was in 2020, after I had published an opinion piece in the *San Antonio Express-News* headlined "Women protect our country, yet military fails to protect them," about my own sexual assault and sexual harassment, that Audrey began to speak to me about what had happened to her.[1] As I spoke up more and more, others began contacting me and sharing their stories.

But it wasn't until we sat down for an interview for this book in 2021 that Audrey opened up and provided the specifics of her experiences. She said it was the first time that she had spoken about it in such detail. No one knew what she was sharing. I felt honored that she trusted me enough to share. During the interview, I had to hide the intense rage I was feeling. Not only was it triggering for me to hear her story, but I wanted somehow to go back in time to defend the young eighteen-year-old airman who had suffered. No one deserves that kind of welcome to the military.

When Audrey arrived at the small overseas base, things initially went quite well. She had her dream job working in OB-GYN. The floor had many women, and the only male was the doctor. She felt comfortable working there, absolutely loved her job, and flourished in her role in medical support. The unit was very nurturing to her in many ways, and she had other women as co-workers and in supervisory roles.

---

1 The piece was republished by *Military Times*, Dec. 2, 2022, as "A call to action: Sexual assault and harassment in the military," https://www.militarytimes.com/opinion/commentary/2020/12/02/a-call-to-action-sexual-assault-and-harassment-in-the-military/.

Everything changed when she was reassigned to another location in the hospital, and not because of the work but because of a sergeant, who pursued her constantly for sex. This sergeant kept after her, saying he could satisfy her sexually. The sexual innuendos, the leering, the constant badgering for sex, were all unrelenting and began to wear her down.

As Audrey spoke through her appalling memories, she constantly slapped the table – whether for emphasis or for reassurance that she was now in control, I don't know. I noticed it in passing during the interview, but hearing it while playing back the audio was striking, even startling. I began to think about it like she was slapping down her harasser.

This sergeant played a role in establishing the work schedule, and she was always put on nights along with him. They were the only two on duty in this department; she was completely isolated from others. Night after night he pursued her, groomed her, and played on her naiveté and vulnerability. It was almost like a form of brainwashing. He continually described in great detail what he was going to do to her sexually, night after night without fail. He was like a calculating predator going after his prey, backing her into a corner to take what he considered his.

As a sergeant much more senior to her, he had total control over her. He knew she was going through a divorce, that her husband had cheated on her, and he used that against her. He was in his forties, she was eighteen, it wasn't even a contest. Eventually he won, and the constant pursuit resulted in sexual activity in their place of work. He did what he said he was going to do to her body. After the first time she dreaded going to work, because she knew what would happen.

It didn't stop until one day when someone questioned why Audrey was always on nights with the sergeant. This is when the chain of command came to her rescue and the wagons circled tightly around Audrey. Her savior was another sergeant, a woman who clearly saw that something was not right. She stepped in and asked Audrey, "Do you feel trapped working on nights with this sergeant? Can you tell me what is going on?" Audrey didn't hesitate to reply. "Oh yeah." She explained exactly what had been occurring. The woman sergeant figured it out. "She could see it," Audrey told me. "She could see that I was frequently on the schedule with him. She asked me what was going on, and I told her the truth." Audrey was scared and feared retribution from the sergeant, but she also felt a huge weight begin to fall away, because now someone knew. Someone could help. However, the shame, embarrassment and self-blame didn't fall off as easily.

She was immediately taken off the shift she had been on. The sergeant was moved and never promoted again. Audrey believes that he received punishment, but she never knew what exactly happened to him. All she knew was that it stopped, and that others created a safe cocoon around her, shielding her from further harm. She was now in the hands of complete professionals, women as well as men of integrity, who protected her for the rest of her time there. She remembers that no one ever formally interviewed her about the situation. Back then there were no formal reporting structures, no sexual assault coordinators. This was the first time that Audrey's chain of command stepped in and handled it right.

The second time occurred at a base in the United States, and once again it involved a sergeant more senior to her. It was at that base that she remarried; she has been happily married for 37 years and has two adult children. Her husband was also in the military. She met him while they were undergoing aeroevac flight training.

At this base, Audrey was openly and brazenly sexually harassed by a higher ranking individual. Several sergeants were in the office discussing getting group tickets to a Cardinals game, as they had done in the past. Audrey said that she and her husband would also like to go and asked for tickets. This higher-ranking sergeant said, "If you want some tickets, you have to put out." Then he leered at her suggestively and left the office. The other sergeant present said, "If you don't say something, I will. We need to do something right now." When they reported this incident to the Officer in Charge (OIC), a major, he looked right at Audrey and said, "You did nothing wrong, and you did not deserve this."

Audrey thinks that the sergeant felt comfortable speaking to her in that manner because he had more rank, and he didn't think she or the other sergeant present would say anything because they all were junior to him. He was that brash. After they reported him, he was removed from his position and received nonjudicial punishment (Article 15).

The result of this whole situation is why Audrey became a first sergeant. Her first sergeant at the time and the entire chain of command just handled it so well; her Shirt especially made sure that the right actions were taken. "I could make a difference by serving as a first sergeant," she concluded.

The sergeant who was fired and disciplined blamed Audrey for his punishment and made sexist comments to her after the incident. Audrey was being groomed for leadership and was now working in the superintendent's office as an assistant. The sergeant told her that the only reason she was in that office was because of what she had done to him, not because of her own potential or merit. "I grew some stones," Audrey told me. "I had some big ass stones." She told him: "You did that to yourself."

She felt the courage to stand up to him because of her chain of command and their support. She also guesses that her husband probably threatened him within an inch of his life. This was a pivotal event for her, feeling that courageous. "Although I was sexually harassed and pursued by predators, the system worked for me in the two instances that I experienced," she says. "My chain of command responded with speed, appropriateness and intolerance towards what occurred."

Audrey remembers that once she became a Shirt, some people treated her differently due to her gender. It was never about just being capable. Her motto was, "Don't ever question my ability to do things or say I can't do it, and don't ever question my integrity." She had to work so much harder to be one step ahead of everyone else. Most people expected the Shirt to be a man and, when they encountered her, she got the typical stereotypes and negative comments about her gender and ability to do the job. Her nickname became the Ice Queen. She relied on her confidence, competence, and perseverence. She *was* the Shirt, and her genuine concern for people always showed through, no matter how difficult the situation was. No one really messed with her after that point.

Looking back, Audrey recalls having great women mentors throughout her military career, and how important they were to her development and sanity. She worked for women at a time when there were so few serving, but their competence, compassion, and leadership all made a huge impression on her.

One case that Audrey dealt with as a Shirt still bothers her to this day. It involved a serial rapist who ended up killing himself after he escaped supervision, denying his six military victims any real justice. This was one case where Audrey says the system failed. As Audrey tells it, "He should have been in pretrial confinement, not under spotty supervision. I advocated for confinement but was overruled. The entire chain of command failed to take the proper action. Those poor victims felt cheated out of justice." Informing them that their rapist had committed suicide was one of the hardest things Audrey has done.

Audrey's experiences in her early career are not unusual. Protect our Defenders points out, in their Facts on United States Military Sexual Violence, that 59 percent of women have been assaulted by someone with a higher rank, and 24 percent were assaulted by someone in their direct chain of command. Sexual harassment victims are at increased risk for sexual assault. One in five women who experience sexual harassment were also sexually assaulted.[2]

What happened to Audrey all those years ago, at her first base, was not her fault. She was targeted, and it was a deliberately, calculated planned campaign that included psychological warfare with an endgame of sexual activity. It was not a situation that she wanted or expected. She was just trying to do her job.

So how has Audrey been able to maintain her sanity and wellness? Through intentional efforts that combine her faith, family, meditation, yoga, walks in nature, lots of self-love, and scuba diving. She says that one must strive to keep all things in balance: spiritual, physical, emotional, and social. She practices what she preaches, with good self-care to keep these and all aspects of her life in sync.

Not only was Audrey successful in the military, she also excelled in higher

---

2 These statistics are from the 2016-2020 Department of Defense Sexual Assault Prevention Response Office report, https://www.sapr.mil/reports.

education and as a contractor. As a university career center director, she created a career closet for students so they could garner high quality suits and other clothing for job interviews and instituted a focused internship coordinator position to help students attain experiential learning. Audrey served as a co-chair for the Veteran Services Advisory Committee while in higher education and excelled at working towards programs and policies that could assist student veterans. She was given a state-level award for her efforts in diversity and for the scope of programming assisting diverse students.

As a contractor with SERCO and the U.S. Department of Labor Veteran Transition Assistance Program, she now assists transitioning service members in navigating employment and career development through in-person and virtual platform learning. She is a purposeful instructor and facilitator, using the sum of all her experiences to help fellow veterans begin their post-military career journey. Always the giver, with a strong sense of helping others, Audrey's mindset is steadfast about service, and this keeps her moving forward and contributing to the success of many.

CHAPTER 4

It's a Man's Navy

JS

My military experiences reflect a true dichotomy, between the really great moments that kept me in the Navy and the darker moments that made it quite challenging to remain.

JS was born and raised in San Francisco, California. She attended college for one semester and worked various odd jobs for a while, but knew she wanted something more in life. San Francisco was expensive, and living with her parents for the rest of her life didn't seem like a viable option.

While working as a waitress, she met several sailors who seemed to have a genuine connection and affinity for each other. She had never seen that type of friendship or bond before. It was the mid-1980s, and they were all male sailors, but they made her feel welcome and were kind to her. They invited her into their circle and took her on a tour of Naval Air Station Alameda. While walking around the pier there, she felt a surreal feeling envelop her and just knew she had a calling to join the Navy.

She experienced such a unique friendship with those sailors and wanted that same kind of camaraderie with others. So a few months later, in 1986, she found herself at seamen recruit training, having enlisted in the Navy. JS found out rather quickly that it was indeed a man's Navy.

JS was born to what back then were called older parents. Her mother was

39 and her father was 44. In fact, her father had served in the Army during World War II. She also had several cousins who served in both the Army and the Air Force, but she was the first among several siblings in her immediate family to join. She told no one that she was joining the Navy. She just did it, took the oath to enter the Delayed Enlistment Program, then sprung the news on the family. Her mother was concerned about her safety; her father more or less offered to help pack her bags. Overall, they were happy for JS to join and proud of her willingness to serve.

JS served twenty years and achieved the grade of E-7 and the rank of Chief Petty Officer. It was a successful career, especially when you consider the era when she joined during and her career field of Aviation Storekeepers (Logistics) and when you become aware of what the environment was like for women in the military then, especially women of color. There was no "political correctness," and it was commonplace to hear men tell inappropriate jokes and make comments and sexual innuendos. There was openly direct flirtation; basically, women got hit on a lot. This seemed to be especially true for the more junior women sailors.

There was no recourse. You really couldn't speak up or report it to anyone; it was just the way it was. These were the times that women found themselves in while serving in a male-dominated military. Either women went along with all the inappropriate comments and jokes, or they faced the consequences. JS knew that speaking out against sexual harassment would have been a career killer. She would have been portrayed as being "too sensitive" or a "troublemaker." Yet she did speak out at times, and she did find herself suffering consequences.

Despite the environment she walked into, JS loved the Navy and became more determined than ever to prove herself. She never wanted to be viewed as someone who couldn't accomplish her duties, so she worked hard, did all the things that were physically challenging, and rarely asked for help, even if it would have been warranted. She wanted to be seen as "one of the guys" and put the mission first above everything. She took on every challenge trying to prove herself, and prove herself she did.

JS describes her time serving as "a true dichotomy, between the really great moments that kept me in the Navy and the darker moments that made it quite challenging to remain."

The great moments included the camaraderie and traveling to new places. It was exciting to change commands every two to four years; she really loved experiencing new people and places. She had an overseas tour to Guam that was great. But perhaps what she liked the very best was her military family. She had several outstanding, strong women role models throughout her time in uniform. These women really stood out for her and inspired her to continue her own leadership journey. Her shipmates were much more than friends; they were like family to her. She had found that unique bond that she had witnessed with those first sailors she had met in San Francisco. The Navy became her second family.

Which is why it pains her so much to reflect on the instances of military sexual trauma that she experienced.

Her first dark moment occurred immediately after she joined, at seamen recruit training, Navy boot camp. Her only previous experience with sailors had been positive and welcoming. So it came as quite a shock when one of the male chiefs at boot camp, not one of her own company commanders (now referred to as recruit division commanders), but another one who had the training rope on his shoulder, groped her. She had never seen him before. He literally walked up to her, while she was standing watch (guard duty) after midnight, and groped her.

This was an E-7, and JS didn't even have rank yet; she was a trainee. She was on duty, standing watch, and out of nowhere came this senior enlisted man. He didn't say anything, just started to grope her. She was absolutely shocked at this behavior. The audacity of his actions was incredible, that he could think it was all right for him to inflict that kind of assault on a very young, vulnerable trainee.

JS recalls that he acted with bravado, that he felt entitled to do what he did. It is impossible to overstate how much positional power and authority this chief had. She just froze, didn't know what to do, and feared reporting the incident. But she knew deep down that it was wrong. And if he could do that to her so brazenly, he had probably done it before and would do it again.

JS suppressed her fear and reported the incident to her company commanders a few days later. These company commanders were like drill sergeants and held a tremendous amount of power over all the trainees. It took momentous courage for her to speak up at boot camp about a chief assaulting her. Many would not have said anything. I know, because I never said anything when it happened to me at Officer Training School.

So how was this sailor's brave act of speaking out dealt with? It wasn't. Not really. One of her company commanders seemed angry at JS. For what? For reporting it, or for waiting several days to report the incident? JS never saw the E-7 perpetrator again and never knew what happened to him, if anything. She assumes that no one ever told her how the situation was disposed of because she was just a trainee. All she knew was that he was a predator; his actions were those of someone who had done such things before, on multiple occasions. JS was never offered any type of counseling. The incident was treated as if it hadn't happened – or at least that was how it seemed like to her. She pressed on, determined to graduate and prove her competence.

She moved on after graduation from boot camp to her first assignment. She describes how, despite always having a bond with her shipmates throughout her career, she knew early on that it was a man's Navy. As a woman – and a woman of color – she really had to work hard to prove she was capable. Questions about her competence always lurked, despite her efforts.

That first assignment was a helicopter squadron. Some of the personnel there came into the unit "undesignated," with no particular assigned role. JS noted that if you were one of the *pretty* girls you were treated differently than the rest. Some of the behavior was subtle, some was more overt. JS picked up on all this. The pretty girls were assigned to office duty jobs and administrative roles; others were sent straight to the line, to work around the aircraft performing maintenance tasks and servicing the aircraft. One pretty girl got a lot of looks, and the men even sang about her. She was blonde and from Georgia, so they sang "Georgia on My Mind."

JS recalls that, less than six months into that first command, still being fairly "green," she did something that one of the senior enlisted was happy about. To let her know he was pleased, he pulled her onto his lap and put his arms around her in front of the whole work center. She even wrote to her father about it, she was so proud of herself. Years later she read that letter and realized how inappropriate that chief's actions were. If it had been a male sailor, surely the chief would not have reacted in the same manner. It was patronizing to her, but that was just the way things were back then.

A more difficult incident occurred when she was an E-5 and stationed on shore duty at a Naval air station on the West Coast. One of the officers there, an O-3, was quite shrewd and old school. He liked JS and felt comfortable making sexual comments to her and about other junior enlisted women sailors. JS remembers that this made her very uncomfortable, and she witnessed his inappropriate behavior quite often. She usually laughed it off, because she really didn't know what else to do.

Toward the end of her tour, she had lunch with a retired chief and confided in him about the experiences surrounding this officer and how it made her feel. Unbeknownst to JS, the retired chief reported it to a woman officer, and somehow the word got back to the officer JS was referring to. Immediately, JS was called into his office and confronted. JS was caught totally off guard, and in that moment she decided to speak up honestly about the way he treated her and other women sailors. She dug deep inside herself just to muster the courage to speak up. She told the officer that his conduct was inappropriate and harassing. She can "still picture his face today as rage filled his eyes," she says. "I felt his contempt for me."

JS recalls feeling that it was her against the world and that nothing would be the same after this. She knew that everything would change, and it did. She felt she had ended up creating a hostile environment for herself, that *she was the one* who had created the hostile environment. The officer ramped up his negative treatment and conduct, making her remaining time there unbearable. At that point in her military career, JS would have gotten out of the Navy if she could have.

JS experienced retaliation for speaking the truth about the harassment she endured and witnessed. Her end of tour Navy and Marine Corps Achievement Medal was downgraded by the officer – the very officer who had harassed her (and other women sailors) and then blamed her for speaking up.

She did not file a formal complaint against the officer, although her male division chief encouraged her to do so. The treatment she had received already was so bad that she feared even more retaliation. Even with her division chief's support, she felt all alone, that it was her against someone who had a tremendous amount of power within the command. Her mind was filled with so many different thoughts: The officer could ruin the rest of her career, other leaders would question why she had tolerated it for so long, and had she maybe even encouraged his behavior in some way?

It came down to his word against hers, and she didn't want to be known as "that female." She simply was not willing to jeopardize her career further or risk additional harassment. She decided that the best way for her to move on was to push it out of her mind. She rationalized: "Outright assault was one thing, but I questioned whether going forward with a sexual harassment claim was worth it."

Unfortunately for JS, in the Navy the word-of-mouth network was alive and well, and she suspected that word had already spread about what had happened on the West Coast. All that toxicity followed her to her new command, where she confronted the same severe level of hostility toward her. She felt like an outsider, never really welcomed into the unit, and everything she did was questioned. The microscope was constantly on her. It was an absolutely terrible year there for JS, under all that scrutiny until a new officer was assigned. He treated her on her merit and her accomplishments and not on her skin color or gender. This command ended up being one of her worst commands but also one of the best, another example of the dichotomy of her service.

JS entered the Navy pre-Tailhook and was serving after that appalling incident, in which 83 women and seven men were assaulted during the 35th Annual Tailhook Symposium in September 1991. Tailhook was an aviators' convention, known as an important gathering over the years where junior officers could interact and engage with senior Naval leaders.[1] The Department of Defense investigated and interviewed thousands of individuals about what had occurred at that 1991 symposium in Las Vegas and compiled numerous pieces of evidence to substantiate the misconduct.

JS believes that, pre-Tailhook, overt harassment, misogyny, and discrimination against women were overt and widespread. Post-Tailhook, those behaviors went more covert and subsided somewhat. For her, it went from lewd jokes and sexual comments openly made in front of her, a total disregard for her feelings and a lack of consideration, to something more subdued. Sadly, JS acknowledges that sexual assault and sexual harassment continued to occur. These types of behaviors, along with the macho military culture, survived Tailhook.

Later in JS's career she served on the command's assessment team, and one of her duties included interviewing victims of sexual harassment. JS was a First Class Petty Officer, and on one occasion she interviewed a junior Second Class Petty officer about her allegations that a male chief in the command had sexually harassed her. Even though this individual had come forward on her own, JS could tell that she was changing her mind about following through with a complaint. It seemed almost déjà vu to JS, as the chief identified as the harasser was well liked and the woman didn't want to be singled out and be put under the microscope.

It was a tough spot to be in, for sure. JS knew firsthand how hard this can be for someone. You don't ever want to be considered not a team player, and to go against the mainstream can be the kiss of death in a variety of ways. All JS could do was collect the facts and not influence her in any way, even though she wanted her to continue with an investigation. She knew all too well what this felt like and related to her not wanting to pursue the incident further. Ultimately, in this case, no official complaint or report was filed.

According to the Department of Defense Annual Report on Sexual Assault in the Military for Fiscal Year 2019 and the 2018 Workplace and Gender Relations Survey of Active Duty Members, "an estimated 24.2 percent of active duty women…indicated experiencing sexual harassment…and

---

1 See "Tailhook '91," https://www.pbs.org/wgbh/pages/frontline/shows/navy/tailhook/91.html.

active duty women who experienced sexual harassment were at three times greater risk for sexual assault than those who did not." The climate within the military is a huge issue as those workplaces with sexual harassment, gender discrimination, or hostility come with significantly increased risk for sexual assault.

As JS moved up the ranks, it seemed to her that the very junior service members didn't know their rights regarding sexual assault and sexual harassment. Some just try to avoid their harassers, which is hard to do since they already stand out as women. For women of color it is even harder to stay under the radar, as it seems you are constantly being watched.

Upon retirement from the Navy, JS dedicated her retirement speech to all the women who had served before her. She really wanted to highlight their sacrifices and thank them for paving the way. In fact, it was a woman in her second command who was an E-7 who had truly taught JS how to be a compassionate leader. Coincidentally, she was also a woman of color. JS's family, her husband and son, also played a strong supportive role.

I asked JS how she coped during her time in the Navy. She said she practiced avoidance but did speak at the time with her boyfriend, who later became her husband. For a long time she would have nightmares of making big mistakes at work and would wake up feeling inadequate and ashamed. Even after retiring from the military, the dreams returned and lasted a few years. She began journaling the dreams and tried to understand what they meant and why she continued to have them. JS had a successful military career, served with honor, was well respected among peers and leaders, and was proud to be a member of the chief petty officer community. So why was she having such dreams? She had nothing to be ashamed about.

She later learned more about trauma and how past traumas resurface and can affect one physically, mentally, and emotionally. While enrolled in a master's counseling and guidance program, she learned about meditation and other positive ways to cope. She had never really dealt with her experiences in the Navy, had pushed those feelings aside, and didn't talk about it. Until she finally began to speak about these incidents in the Navy, fifteen years later, she never realized that she had harbored such strong emotions.

She now understands that she was made to feel like an "other," that she had no agency and her voice didn't matter. Once she remembered her experiences and acknowledged them, coupled with self-care methods, she has been able to let go of those old feelings. Still, JS says, "There's that little, tiny, almost whisper in the back of my mind that questions whether I did something wrong." Now much stronger, she has since learned the power of saying no to anything that is incongruent with her values.

JS shared her coping methods with me and recommended that I read *The Body Keeps the Score* by Bessel Van Der Kolk, M.D. That book was a game changer for me, and I am so very grateful to JS. It helped me connect all the dots on my trauma and how it has impacted my body, mind, and brain. I now understand much better the linkages between trauma and its impact on me.

JS has a master's degree in counseling and guidance and a bachelor's degree in organizational leadership. She uses her experience and education to help others, something she is quite passionate about. She worked previously as a clinical therapist but now focuses more on the military affiliated community: both those currently serving and retired personnel, and their families. She provides advocacy, peer to peer mentoring, and support services and approaches her work from a holistic framework, as she knows that you must help military affiliated community members in a multi-faceted approach. One initiative rarely works by itself; it takes a combined, supportive network to truly make a difference in the lives and families of those who served the country.

JS is a confident woman who reflects on her lived military experiences as both the best of times and the worst of times, just like life. She has learned much in her time on this earth as a woman, a woman of color, and a Navy veteran. She shares her truth to assist others. She stands up, speaks up, and takes agency for herself. No one can take that from her. Not anymore.

CHAPTER 5

DOUBLE STANDARDS

Jennifer Suarez Lugo

My family always came first. This was extremely difficult as I struggled balancing my career with my family while serving, especially when I became a single parent. I know it affected my assignments and my climb up the ladder.

Many women struggle achieving rank in the military, balancing family with the mission. Jennifer Suarez-Lugo was no different than most. However, she found a way and excelled at both, earning a Bronze Star medal for her accomplishments in combat in Iraq and an appointment as a squadron commander. This came at a heavy cost to her, both physically and emotionally. It also speaks volumes to the kind of person Jen is.

She climbed that ladder, first as a young enlisted troop in the Army, then later as an officer in the Air Force. What makes her climb to success all that more significant is that she is a woman of color (Latina), came from very humble beginnings, and overcame extreme hardships growing up. Despite the odds against her, she went on to be the first in her family to get a college degree and to become a commissioned officer in the military. But her journey to become an officer was not linear; it came with off ramps in and out of college and the military.

What also makes her rise in the military so important is that she accomplished it while enduring sexual harassment. Her service was filled with outstanding experiences, but also came with sacrifice. Jen says she experienced various forms of sexual harassment during her service in the Army and the Air Force, with the most substantial occurring while in the Army. Jen recalls gender discrimination, stalking, sexualized language, gestures, and behaviors. At times she was in a hostile, intimidating and offensive work environment, and still she prevailed.

To put her successes throughout her life in perspective, it is helpful to learn more about Jen's background. Her grandparents were migrant workers, making the long trek from South Texas to Michigan each year to pick crops. One year her grandfather became ill, and the family ended up staying in Michigan. Jen was born there, in Saginaw, to very young parents. Her mother was just 15 when she became pregnant with Jen, and her father was 19. Her father was from South Texas and was the youngest of 12 children. Her mother was from Michigan and the third child out of four. They married, living together for only a year before divorcing.

Mother and daughter sort of grew up together. When Jen was three her mom was eighteen, and by then a brother had come along. They became welfare kids and lived in Section 8 housing on government assistance. Their mother did what she could to support them and returned to school to get her GED. Jen's mother taught her early on the importance of an education, and she learned that lesson well. That early hard living helped drive Jen to do more and achieve more.

Despite the meager conditions they lived in, the home she grew up in never lacked for love. She was told every day that she was loved. Sadly, when Jen was quite young, she was sexually abused for several years, and the trauma she suffered shaped how she would come to view herself and thus impacted her entire life. Despite the horrific abuse she suffered, it never curtailed her *ganas*, the inner desire to better herself and to achieve success, whatever that might look like.

Her mom's remarriage when Jen was eleven grew the family into a large blended one, and Jen found herself with six siblings split across her father's new family and her stepfather's family. She says that she views all of them as her brothers and sisters; they are one big family and are connected.

Jen was active in both middle and high school, participating in band and working various jobs to help out the family. She was a good student, but not the greatest student. She applied herself and began dreaming of being the first in the family to go to college. "I only knew two things back then," she told me. "One was that I wanted to leave home in search of a better life and two, that I was broke."

She asked her mother for help, but her mother said she had no idea how to navigate the college application process. Plus, her mother was very busy working and raising a toddler. She wanted to help, just didn't know how. So on her own Jen started researching the financial aid process and speaking with counselors. Her stepdad drove her to visit several campuses.

First-generation students who attend college know all too well how intimidating the entire process can be, from initial acceptance to financial aid forms and scholarship applications. It can be a daunting process, even with help. It was not easy for Jen; this was a world she knew nothing about. She knew, though, that "with God's help and determination that it would all work out." And it did: She graduated from high school in 1987 and was accepted into Michigan State University on a full financial aid package, which speaks volumes about her perseverance and *ganas*.

Her world got that much bigger as she was exposed to different peoples and cultures while attending Michigan State. She recalls that out of about 49,000 students, there were fewer than 200 Hispanic/Latino students and around 500 African American students. Although in the two years she attended she participated in student groups and was an active student, she still felt isolated and out of place, even with assistance provided for minority students.

She came home after her sophomore year of college, began contemplating her life, and ended up determining that she just wasn't mature enough to stay in school. Besides, she was just tired of school. "I met a cute Army recruiter and my life changed," she laughs. "Doesn't everyone who served have a story about their recruiter?" Hers was particularly astute, as he asked her what no one ever had: "If you could do anything with your life, what would it be?"

"I told him I wanted to learn fluent Spanish and utilize that skill, and if the military could do that for me, then I was all in," she told me.

Her family didn't really believe she was serious about joining the military, but she was, and the recruiter was able to get her lined up with the exact position she was interested in, as a Cryptologist Linguist (Spanish). He also helped her get into shape, lose weight, and withdraw from the university. "I just knew I had to find out more about what the world had to offer and what I could offer the world." She enlisted into the Army in 1989 with two years of college under her belt, but she was scared, as she knew her goal of always staying under the radar, not being noticed, was not going to bode well in basic training and in the Army.

She flourished at basic training, and for the first time in her life discovered a confidence she never knew existed. She was surprised at what she was able to do physically, marveling at her own achievements, could shoot a gun, pump out pushups with ease, could run like never before. Everything they threw at her she could handle. She became a badass, a *chingona*. The Army broke her down and built her back up.

Jen was so engrossed in her training at boot camp that she wasn't aware, until she was close to graduating, how some of the training instructors were interacting with other women recruits. Several were having sex with them. She began to hear whispers of what was occurring, how some of the drill instructors were actively seeking out women to sleep with, finding the most vulnerable and leveraging their positions of power.

Sickened by this behavior, she remembers how cold and calculating their targeting was. It was a real eye-opener for her and brought back horrible memories of her own sexual abuse by someone in a position of power when she was a child. Fortunately for Jen, she never experienced any type of sexual assault at boot camp. Although she excelled there, she did endure – like most of the women – elements of sexual harassment like cat calls, and sexual innuendos which sort of came with the territory.

Staying off anyone's radar at basic was difficult, as women stood out from the male trainees. An incident occurred that directly involved Jen during basic training, regarding learning how to rappel. She was so excited about trying something new and edgy. When it was her turn to come down the wall another trainee yelled out that one of the sergeants held Jen's ropes. "I instantly got scared," she told me. "He was very old school, always walked around with a snarl on his face. Just as I was about to rappel down, he grabbed my safety rope and pulled it up as hard as he could between my legs. It scared the hell out of me and hurt so much." She got down as quickly as she could to get away from him. He said something snide to her as she walked past him. Jen believes that he hated seeing women in the military and purposefully acted the way he did towards them.

Jen received technical training, or advanced individual training (AIT), at cryptology school at Goodfellow AFB, Texas. While there she had an incident with another student. She went out with him once or twice and thought nothing of it; she was single and could date as she pleased. He was in her same training and seemed okay. At first.

According to Jen, he ended up being a creep who stalked and harassed her. He spread all kinds of untruths about her and their supposed relationship. He told anyone who would listen that they were engaged and would marry. As Jen tells it, he created this entire story about them and repeatedly told people that he was in love with her and that she loved him too. Jen reported his behavior, as she understood it was harassment and it frightened her. Initially the instructor didn't believe her, thought she couldn't be serious. Per Jen, everyone believed the male who was harassing her, no one believed her except for her enlisted peers. The leadership did not.

Jen reports that he stalked her for at least a month and made her life miserable. She kept telling him no, but he just didn't get it. He believed they were in love. The leadership ended up moving Jen out of the flight. Basically, they moved the person they perceived as the problem. "They moved me. He got to stay in the same flight. This is the double standard that occurs for men and women in situations like these: The men are usually believed over the women." It was a long five months going through advanced training with him there.

How ironic that Jen had left college because she was sick of going to school, and then the Army put her through an entire year of schools and training so she could be qualified in her career field. Finally done with all her training, she headed overseas to Panama for her first assignment and participated in joint operations with other services. Life was good, she loved the Army, had a real mission, and was surrounded by a lot of Hispanic/Latino enlisted personnel, largely due to the career field she was in as a Spanish linguist.

One night she got a Red Cross message that her grandmother was dying back in Michigan. The military typically helps in such situations and tries to get you back home. Jen was quite upset when she heard about her grandmother's deteriorating condition. She had been working administrative CQ duty (charge of quarters) and was staffing the desk for the barracks.

Jen was amped up, antsy. She was leaving first thing the next morning, but decided to stay on duty that night. She was alone at the desk, concerned about her grandmother, visibly upset. Jen was an E-3 at the time, and a male sergeant senior to her came in. It was close to 2 a.m. She wasn't alarmed as she knew him, considered him a friend, and trusted him. When she told him about her grandmother, he didn't offer any condolences or words of encouragement. Instead, Jen says he just looked at her and proceeded to tell her what he wanted to do to her sexually. In detail, he explicitly described how he wanted to undress her and what sexual acts he wanted to commit on her body.

Totally shocked, Jen looked directly at him and said, "I just told you my grandmother is dying, and here you are hitting on me." She says he just stared at her and then abruptly left. Jen said it was all so bizarre, he was supposed to be a friend, he was married with children and had been selected for promotion. He was a golden boy. Once Jen returned from her grandmother's funeral, she started getting creepy, graphic, and disturbing letters from this sergeant, the ones that use letters cut out from magazines and newspapers. Jen couldn't believe it and says it was almost like out of a movie. She was upset and shaken by this, so she just tried to avoid him.

But she could hardly do that; they worked together. She was clearly intimidated by her stalker/perpetrator. This sergeant outranked her and had a slot for a significant promotion in the Army. Her boyfriend and roommate both told her to report him and they gave her the courage to report the incidents. What happened? They changed her shift and gave him a no contact order (to stay away from Jen), but still allowed him to get promoted and undergo advanced training. That just didn't sit right with Jen. With higher rank, he would have even more power and could potentially target other women. "I felt like they were rewarding his bad behavior, it was always the woman's fault," she says.

It's just like before at AIT, Jen thought. It's that double standard that exists in the military between how men and women are treated whenever an incident occurs. "The women were always considered the Jezebels out of these situations," she says. "We get called sluts, whores, it is always our fault, never the guys. They leverage their positions of power over women. Although my enlisted supervisor reported it up the chain and a no contact order was issued, the officer leadership still allowed the perpetrator to continue advancing. All he really got was a slap on the wrist."

Jen got out of the Army because she believed she could do more. As an enlisted troop she was always told what to do and understood that they didn't welcome initiative. "The Army is very good about telling you how they want things done. So, if you go outside of that box you get in trouble. I think I am smart enough to figure things out and have a lot to contribute." It was time to go back to school and get that degree, so she got out of the Army as an E-5 sergeant. She started working and attending community college. She had a new mission. It was 1993.

When she had served in the Army, she had thought the Air Force personnel were really cool, and in the early 1990s the Air Force was actively trying to bring in more diverse recruits through their college and university Reserve Officer Training Corps (ROTC) programs. Jen completed her associate's degree from Central Texas College and garnered a competitively sought walk-on slot to attend ROTC's summer field training. At this point she wasn't associated with any particular ROTC program at any four-year college.

Once she completed the training as a distinguished graduate, she selected the Air Force's Detachment 842 at The University of Texas at San Antonio graduating in two years and entering the Air Force as an officer with the career field of her choice, Personnel (similar to HR work, but with an entire range of duties in combat). She purposely didn't select something similar to what she had done in the Army; she really wanted something different for her new leadership role.

The differences between serving as an enlisted troop in the Army and as an officer in the Air Force were stark. First, there was very little diversity in the Air Force. In the Army as an enlisted troop there were more diverse people, especially in her field as a Spanish linguist. She was around lots of Hispanic/Latino troops, although not many officers. In the Air Force, there were hardly any Hispanic/Latino airmen serving, and that made her feel out of place.

This reminded Jen of her first two years of college: the isolation and loneliness as a Latina among so many white people. And the fact that there were so few women only compounded these feelings. "There was an added pressure to make sure you always looked good," she told me, "because if you do not, they are going to remember if you had an off day. There were very few Hispanic officers on any base at any given time. I mean, that is still probably true to this day."

Second, she got married a year after joining the Air Force. There were indeed differences between being a young single woman serving and being a married woman with children. She is fond of saying that she had three children back-to-back-to-back. Which made it all that much harder as an officer with the responsibilities of being a leader, staying in shape, and enduring the operations tempo that serving in very demanding positions can have. "My family always came first," says Jen. "This was extremely difficult as I struggled balancing my career with my family while serving, especially when I became a single parent. I know it affected my assignments and my climb up the ladder."

Third, serving as an officer in the Air Force was totally different from the Army regarding thinking outside the box, innovation, and creativity. These traits that Jen says were not welcome for a young, enlisted troop in the Army were lauded and highly encouraged in the Air Force as an officer. She thrived in that type of culture.

Jen's first assignment as an officer was as a gold bar recruiter. It was part of a program to help bring in more diversity, where newly minted second lieutenants would assist in the recruitment of minorities as officers. Ironic that she helped to bring in more underrepresented individuals to try to diversify the Air Force, but as she navigated her own officer career she found few Hispanic/Latino officers. She adds that in her entire military career of more than 25 years, she never saw or met a Latina that was a full colonel other than me.

Serving as an officer wasn't always easy for her. Jen says she disliked the politics that she witnessed in the Air Force among the officer corps and the leadership. "It definitely wasn't as much fun as being enlisted," she says. "You have more people staring at you, constantly measuring you. I've always been a curvy girl. Sometimes I felt like I just was being judged all the time. It was exhausting."

After a year of specialized recruiting duty, she found herself in Germany, at an aircraft maintenance squadron that had few women or Hispanic/Latino individuals. She found herself trying to keep up with all the work, staying in shape, and caring for her family. There were many times she would wake at 0430, go to the gym, come home to get the kids ready for school, then head off to a ten-hour workday. Then rush to pick up the kids and go back to work to finish up some lingering paperwork or projects.

Life was fast-paced. It became increasingly difficult for Jen to find time to work out to meet standards. She was not naturally physically fit and struggled to meet standards. "I've always been a shorter curvy girl and after having my kids, it was really hard to get back within weight and physical fitness standards," she says.

She recalls being on diet pills on and off throughout her military career, chasing that elusive image for her of looking sharp in uniform. She felt the constant burden of being under the microscope, being watched, being judged as a woman and a Latina. Jen believed that a double standard existed between men and women when it came to working out and using duty time to do so. "When you are a woman and you take your time to go to the gym, you get flak for it, but no one thinks twice about the men spending a couple of hours there," she asserts. "I always had to be better and more competitive than everyone else."

She experienced some characteristics of what is referred to as body dysmorphia. It wasn't until much later that she began to connect her thoughts and emotions about her appearance and body to the sexual abuse she had suffered as a child.

Jen says this also impacted how she wanted to fly under the radar, to be somewhat invisible. She always worked hard, but at the same time she didn't want to be noticed. That was virtually impossible in the Air Force; the higher ranked she became, the more she stood out as a leader. She believes that her curviness kept her from some selective assignments, like working in protocol with very senior officers.

Jen was stationed at the Air Force Academy in 2004, during a tumultuous time following a sexual assault scandal that took place there the year before. It was horrific in the number and scale of the assaults and harassment and the alleged cover-ups that ensued.[1] Four senior officers, to include the superintendent of the academy, were ultimately removed and transferred elsewhere in the service, but they were not discharged.

The scandal was brought to light after more than 60 current and former female cadets came forward reporting rapes and other abuse at the academy.[2] Jen was a section commander but was soon given an adjunct role as a deputy sexual assault response coordinator (SARC), to assist victims and to help execute their newly created SARC program and other policies included in the Agenda for Change, which was the mandate the academy was operating under when she arrived. Jen was there when the infamous sign that read "Bring Me Men" was replaced with the Air Force's core values.

Later in Jen's military career, she was selected as a commander. This is a

---

1 For additional information please refer to the Office of the Inspector General of the Department of Defense Report No. IP02004C003, December 3, 2004, *Evaluation of Sexual Assault, Reprisal, and Related Leadership Challenges at the United States Air Force Academy*, https://media.defense.gov/2018/Oct/19/2002053445/-1/-1/1/IPO2004C003-REPORT%20(SECURED).PDF

2 "Air Force leadership blamed for sex scandal," *Chicago Tribune*, September 23, 2003, https://www.chicagotribune.com/news/ct-xpm-2003-09-23-0309230296-story.html

huge leadership accomplishment, as it is highly competitive. When she became a commander her struggles with being the center of attention became all too real and difficult for her. "I was scared, really out of my mind," she recalls. "I didn't want to be noticed, and it intimidated me." But she did her job to the best of her ability and left command decorated with a meritorious service medal.

Jen's third overseas assignment was to Iraq in 2009. She spent a year deployed at FOB Shield in Sadr City, in eastern Baghdad. It was a small base and had contractors, state department, and different services all working there. She recalls that there were gender issues serving in that combat environment, so she hung with a small core group of fellow Air Force officers who had each other's back in that tough environment. She got hit on a lot, as did most of the few women that were there. They got hit on by all the men, particularly by contractors. One contractor banged on her door one evening asking her for money. She didn't believe he was trying to sexually assault her, but she was scared all the same.

One of the Iraqi officers hit on her. She was able to keep him and the contractors away and stick with her core Air Force people, but it was a constant battle in an environment that had its own challenges.

Jen earned a Bronze Star for her achievements in Iraq as Deputy Director, Human Resources, Iraq Training and Advisory Mission-Ministry of Interior under the Multi-National Security Transition Command-Iraq. Her efforts leading a multidisciplinary team of military officers, contractors, and local national translators demonstrated leadership and maturity beyond the rank that she held. In fact, according to her citation, she "planned, coordinated, and executed over 30 missions outside the joint security station, and served daily under high threat of improvised explosive devices, and direct fire attacks." Her leadership skills were put to the test in the most extreme environment for military members and she excelled, never backing down from responsibility. As military and first responders are apt to do, this Latina ran towards danger not away, never hesitating. Jen overcame adversity, persevered, and earned the prestigious Bronze Star medal for her efforts.

I met Jen when she was being reassigned out of Iraq. I interviewed her to work in the very same ROTC detachment that she graduated and commissioned from all those years ago. I was the commander and needed to fill a position among my cadre staff. Who I put in front of young, impressionable cadets was important to me. I wanted the right officer, the best role model. To this day I know I made the right decision putting Jen in the detachment. She was the perfect role model, as her background was similar to many of our cadets. The University of Texas at San Antonio is a Hispanic Serving Institution, and the AF ROTC detachment was rich with diverse cadets, just like the student body as a whole. Jen was a Latina like many of the cadets, was always real to them, and never carried herself with anything but professionalism.

She ended up retiring as a lieutenant colonel in the Air Force, after getting out of the Army as an E-5 sergeant, serving a combined service of 26 years. She was successful despite her humble beginnings and early child sexual abuse and the isolation and harassment she endured in the military.

Overall, Jen loved the military. She especially liked traveling, expanding her horizons, meeting people she might never have met, and the educational opportunities. She has made lifelong friendships and bonds with many she served with and keeps in touch with them to this day. She truly did find another familia within the military.

She continues to give back as a civilian for the Air Force, as she now works within AF ROTC providing oversight and guidance. Almost like going full circle. She makes decisions that impact other young ROTC cadets and works hard to ensure diversity among the officer ranks.

Jen speaks up about her experiences in the hopes of educating others and to inform many that they are not alone in whatever they have experienced or still are experiencing. Life has not been easy for Jen, but she knows how to make it work, helping herself and others at the same time.

Regarding sexual assault and sexual harassment, she says she is "proud to be part of change! A taboo subject that must be tackled head on." I am proud to be a mentor to her, and grateful to her for being courageous and speaking out about the traumas she experienced and the tough aspects of her life. "As I have said before, I'd do anything for my family," Jen says. "My service was worth the sacrifice."

I asked Jen just how she coped all those years serving, indeed how she still copes. She says that she has been in and out of therapy her entire life. All those years of feeling bad about her appearance and her body have worn on her. She has written a little about her experiences, but has yet to decide what to do with her writings. Perhaps one day she will share them with us, as I imagine they will have a profound and lasting impact.

CHAPTER 6

THE GREATER GOOD

Tammy I. Barlet

The instances that occurred when I was being sexually harassed or experienced outright sexism were so shocking in that no one ever said anything at the time or later. Not one person ever stepped up to my aid. I had to face each situation alone.

Tammy Barlet joined the Coast Guard at age 18, right out of high school. She made up her mind to join at 17 and had to get her parents to sign for her. No one in her immediate family had ever served in the military. Some extended family members had served in the military, but none in the Coast Guard. She would become the sole "coastie."

So, why did she join? "In my small town in Pennsylvania the options after high school were few," she says. "Basically I could go to college, raise a family and work, or join the military."

She was influenced by a few things. First, she knew she couldn't support herself to go to college. Second, she fondly remembered times spent on the water with her family in Delaware and observing the Coast Guard there. Third, she saw an ad for the Coast Guard in a magazine and was intrigued. She laughs and says that coastie recruiters never actually came to her high school, but the television show *Baywatch*, which featured lifeguards and coasties saving people, was popular at that time, in 1995. So she just called the Coast Guard 1-800 number to learn more.

Tammy wanted to be part of an organization whose main mission was to help those in need. The Coast Guard's mission of search and rescue seemed to be just what she needed and wanted. She had taken the ASVAB (Armed Services Vocational Aptitude Battery exam) and scored well enough to be guaranteed a specific geographical area to be assigned to. She selected the region including southern New Jersey, Maryland, Delaware, and Virginia, as she wanted to stay close to home.

But she had to get her parents' permission to serve, since she was not old enough to commit on her own even though she would be turning eighteen a month before starting boot camp – just a month and a half after completing high school. The recruiter informed her parents that she would be safe and that she could stay stateside. Famous last words. Throughout her eight years of service she was underway in many overseas locations, to include the Persian Gulf, and experienced many port calls in foreign lands. But her parents couldn't know that then, and they gave their permission.

Tammy attended enlisted basic training for the Coast Guard at Training Center Cape May, New Jersey. According to the Coast Guard, Cape May is the single accession jumping off point for the entire coastie enlisted force. Basic training is a challenging environment physically, academically, and mentally. Tammy received small arms and seamanship training, along with firefighting and damage control instruction. The training companies were co-ed, but the sleeping quarters were not. She remembers being pushed by her company commanders to be as good as the guys, if not better.

Tammy wasn't what you would call naturally physically fit. Although she pumped out the required sit-ups, push-ups, and swim standards relatively easily, she had to push herself to the brink to pass the mile-and-a-half run. She recalls other women who ran faster running alongside her to encourage her. The day they all took the run for qualifying, she did her best.

The senior company commander had her believing that she did not make the standard, so at the end of the run she thought she had not passed. No one said anything when she crossed the finish line, so she really believed that she hadn't made it and would either be washed back to start training again or kicked out. She ran into the barracks, visibly upset. The senior company commander followed her and, Tammy recalls, "He comes screaming through the barracks saying, 'Why are you crying, why are you upset? You passed!'" Of course she was elated, but those mind games certainly were nerve racking.

One night while Tammy was standing watch duty alone at basic, one of the company commanders approached her and asked what she would do if someone attacked her. "Sir, I would yell for help," Tammy replied. He stopped her then and there and said, "You need to yell 'Fire,' not 'Help.' People will respond faster that way. You might not get help if you yell 'Help.'" This piece of advice scared her a little and was something Tammy never forgot, especially as a woman in a male-dominated military.

After basic, Tammy got her geographic location but not her preferred career field of serving as a corpsman (similar to medical tech). This was partly due to there not being many positions available for women in the Coast Guard and that the corpsman training school had a three-year wait. Her first duty station ended up being in Virginia at a support center handing out basketballs and cleaning gum off bleachers. Not very exciting or glamorous to Tammy. She knew she couldn't keep that up for three years waiting for her training slot.

So, after six months of doing what seemed like meaningless labor, she approached her chief and asked what could be done. He provided career advice and discussed her going to radarman school, since she had done so well on her ASVAB and that particular rating (career field) was the only one with an immediate opening at the time. So she went to radarman advancement training in Yorktown and became qualified in the rating.

Ironic how just the title of her rating sounded masculine, and she was reminded daily that, as a woman, she was indeed a minority while serving. The title of her rating didn't change until 2003, her last year of service, when several ratings were combined to form the operations specialist, the radarman rating merging with the quartermaster and telecommunications ratings.

After Yorktown she was on her way to Alaska to meet her ship, USCGC *Chase* (a high endurance cutter), which was basically floating search and rescue stations for the crabbing and fishing fleet in the Bering Sea. She couldn't wait to get underway and make a difference as a coastie.

But being stuck at that support center for her first duty station had put her behind her peers, who had already been underway at sea gaining valuable experience. She was an E-3 when she finally got to a ship, and her learning curve was straight up. There was no time to waste. She had to learn fast, but she was ready. This was what she had dreamed of for so long: to serve at sea.

Tammy served on a cycle of three months on patrol, then back at home port in Long Beach for three months upgrading systems and overhauling the ship, then back underway again to do another three-month patrol. She was on three Alaska patrols. She also went to Thailand for four months assisting the Royal Thai Navy and visited several Thai ports. The *Chase* conducted military interdiction operations in the Persian Gulf for six months. During these operations, Tammy assisted in the seizure of fuel oil of over 1.5 million gallons, diverted four vessels violating United Nations sanctions against Iraq, and participated in 85 gunnery exercises.

While in the Persian Gulf, she served on Charlie duty watch sections, which had her on duty for six hours performing air direction controlling, then off for twelve hours. She would set up the flight briefings and, once the helicopter/aircraft left the ship, was responsible for the communications between the ship and the aircraft. She communicated with any United States aircraft that came into her ship's air zone, inquiring about how many souls on board, how much fuel they had, as they flew to and from their mission. Once the aircraft left her airspace, another ship's operational specialist would take over.

It was demanding duty and tasking for anyone, but once she completed her air direction duties, she didn't really get to take those full twelve hours off, as she also had specialized training in intel gathering. So every time the helicopters went up, she would go with them to gather photographic, audio, and video intel. There were times they came across boats and had to engage to determine if they were friend or foe. At least two times, incoming fire came close to the *Chase*, but there were no outright attacks on her.

Tammy says she experienced sexual harassment, outright sexism, and ageism. "I was fortunate that I only experienced what I did," she says. "It could have been much worse." Aboard ship, a petty officer who was supposed to be her mentor refused to perform that role and never provided her guidance or the training she needed. According to Tammy, he tried to sabotage her advancement and career development.

She worked in the Combat Information Center aboard ship and recalls that initially there was one other woman besides her in the department. Once this other woman departed, things became much more difficult for Tammy. As the only woman, she began to see how one particular shipmate really felt and acted towards her. "He clearly did not want women in the military and believed I was too young to serve in my position and in supervisory roles," she recalls.

When she was up for advancement from watch stander to watch supervisor, Tammy says she experienced overt sexism. Typically, one is assigned an individual to help train and prepare one for going before the advancement board. However, no one had taken on that role or been assigned specifically to Tammy. She was on her own. The other members of the board all supported and prepped her as much as they could, although they had other individuals they were responsible for. After all, it was her supervisor's responsibility to do this for her.

Nonetheless, on the day of the board, all the members voted to advance her further to watch supervisor. Except for one particular shipmate. Tammy recalls exactly what he said at that board: He said that he "could not vote to advance her due to her age and gender," that "the role was just too important." She was stunned, as she firmly believed that he had just discriminated against her due to her age and gender. She sat in silence and observed all the other board members, who said not one word. Not one person spoke up on her behalf or about what had just been said. You could hear the sounds of the ship, but not one voice spoke.

At the time, Tammy didn't even think about reporting formally what had occurred. There were two women officers within the department, but to Tammy they didn't seem approachable. Plus, she still felt that the harassment should be dealt with inside her department. This was extremely difficult, though, given that the particular shipmate was in her same department. She felt alone and isolated.

The board did advance her forward to the role of watch supervisor, so she didn't experience retaliation in the traditional sense. But she felt as if the scrutiny she was under became even more intense, and the harassment escalated. She became hyperaware, as she knew he was watching and waiting for her to fail. Tammy believes that this particular shipmate really upped his game of harassment after she had been advanced to watch supervisor. "I had to make sure all my Ts were crossed and I's were dotted," she says. "There was no room for any kind of error on my part."

Another time, this same shipmate stated in front of others, "I know you are interested in how long it is," she knew he wasn't talking about the duty day. His sexual innuendo was obvious and directed pointedly at her. Tammy was just twenty years old at this time. She stood there, awestruck, and looked around the room, really hoping that one of the five or six other men there would speak up. No one said a word.

"The instances that occurred when I was being sexually harassed or experienced outright sexism were so shocking in that no one ever said anything at the time or later," Tammy recalls. "No one person ever stepped up to my aid. I had to face each situation alone."

The sexualized and inappropriate remarks continued. Tammy says that, after it happened at least five more times, she had just had it and blurted out, "Don't talk to me like that. You don't talk to anyone else like that. If you can't talk properly, then don't talk at all." This took a tremendous amount of courage on her part, not only because he was in a position of authority and senior to her, but because she had blurted it out in front of others. Would she gain allies after defending herself by speaking up, or would she gain enemies amidst her brothers in arms? Since the harassment didn't stop, one can guess that she didn't win many allies. She was at her wits' end.

So she took it up the chain of command to her chief, informing him that they worked behind locked doors in a small space, and that he was always there, harassing her. "I am in a vulnerable position. I enjoy my job, enjoy being on ship, but I cannot work with him," she admitted. Did her chief have her back? No. According to Tammy, her chief said, "He is a senior petty officer with over fifteen years. Don't ruin this man's career." No one seemed to care what Tammy thought, or how she felt working day in and day out in that environment.

Tammy described enduring relentless harassment, gender discrimination, and ageism by someone more senior to her on the ship and getting no relief after reporting it. She couldn't escape it; aboard ship she lived and worked in a toxic environment. For three years. The only time she had a bit of relief was when another woman worked in her same department, but that was for a short period.

When I asked her why some of the others never said anything, she says that everyone seemed to care only about the men and their feelings. "The younger guys around me felt threatened," she added. "They didn't speak up. They were worried about themselves, retaliation, and their own careers."

Conversely, when I asked Tammy what the best part of serving was, her face lit up as she fondly recalled her involvement helping others less fortunate. She loved that she could help others with humanitarian aid around the world. As president of the enlisted MWR (morale, welfare and recreation) aboard the ship, she organized many events at almost every port call. Examples included providing teddy bears to medical service groups in the area for children hospitalized in Australia, delivering supplies and toiletries in Guatemala and on Guam, supporting aid to orphanages in the form of painting, and playing soccer with kids. Tammy not only led these efforts but happily participated in each one.

In fact, she wasn't content with just doing her military service to help those in need, search and rescue, and immigrant assistance. She went beyond that with her own volunteer service. "I knew I would always be doing something for the greater good and this was one of the main reasons I joined the Coast Guard," she told me. She continued her service when she was landlocked at a home station, volunteering at hospitals and horse ranches. She credits her parents with showing her what service to and for others is all about.

While at one port call, she and several other coasties were authorized 24 hours on land. Off they went to explore the area and let off steam. Upon their return, it appeared that one of them had not been authorized to stay overnight on land and was administratively punished with nonjudicial punishment, what is referred to in the Coast Guard as a captain's mast.

Unfortunately, Tammy got lumped in with what had happened, and even though she had been authorized to be off ship overnight, her and another friend were charged with fraternization and also met a captain's mast. "No one really listened to my side or believed me that my male married friend and I were just friends and didn't even stay in the same hotel room while off ship," she told me. "In fact, I shared a room off base that night with another woman coastie." This situation occurred while she was still undergoing harassment from that one particular petty officer. She wasn't surprised that he didn't listen to her explanation of events. Fortunately, she wasn't reduced in rank and was only assigned extra duty. Tammy says he was always lurking around, just waiting for her to make a mistake.

In 2001 Tammy was in a serious service-connected accident that was career-ending. She had just made Sailor of the Quarter, and things were going fairly well for her. She was in the hospital for two weeks and on medical leave for four months. She was able to return to her landlocked duty station, but couldn't be aboard ship anymore due to her injuries. Since she was close to separation, she extended her contract for six months, then on a month-to-month basis until she was finally able to meet a medical board to determine fitness for duty and disability.

This was a very stressful time, being on pins and needles about the outcome of a board that had lifelong implications. She was afraid to speak to anyone about the severity of the depression that she was going through, as she knew what that ultimately could do to her clearance status. Her supervisor – not the same one that had been on ship – encouraged her to speak to someone. She tried talk therapy during her last few months on active duty. She ended up with a medical separation or discharge and not a medical retirement. She firmly believes it should have been a medical retirement from the very beginning.

After leaving the service, Tammy went on unemployment for six months and begin to contemplate her future. She ended up marrying the first man that paid any real attention to her and that marriage lasted less than five years.

Tammy hit a mental wall and was in a bad place; her work was not great, no real advancement, her marriage was terrible, and a relative had just died by suicide. The loss by suicide was that much more detrimental to Tammy because she had another relative who died by suicide while serving in the military. She knew she needed help and saw a psychologist, who really didn't engage with her, just prescribed medication. She told her primary care doctor, "I need something more than meds." This was a huge step for Tammy. Asking for help is not easy for veterans. She started getting some real mental health assistance, and she gives credit to the social worker she worked with for basically saving her life.

She turned her life around, went to school, and became active on campus with the Student Veterans of America (SVA). This was a big deal as Tammy was one of many women veterans who didn't identify as veterans. As a woman veteran myself, a higher education professional, and the founder of a veteran and military affairs department at a university, I have seen this lack of self-reporting by women student veterans. Current research exists to substantiate that this might be due to the sexual assault, sexual harassment, and gender discrimination that some women vets endured while serving.

According to Dr Vanessa Meade, professor of social work at the University of Alaska and a veteran herself, in the *Journal of Veterans Studies*, "Women's identity as veterans interlocks with the sexism and gender bias that permeates our society and particularly in the hypermasculinity of military culture."[1] Some women veterans simply do not want to be reminded of what they might have endured while serving, and Tammy fell into that category after leaving the Coast Guard. It wasn't until she started going to college, ten years after departing military life, that she began to acknowledge her service.

Tammy thrived in school, ending up getting a bachelor's in public health from Temple University and a Master of Public Health degree from George Washington University. In 2019, she also participated in the prestigious and competitive VFW-SVA Legislative Fellowship Program. She now oversees

---

1 Meade, Vanessa, "Embracing Diverse Women Veteran Narratives: Intersectionality and Women Veteran's Identity," *Journal of Veterans Studies*, vol. 6 no. 3 (2020), pp. 47-53, https://journal-veterans-studies.org/article/10.21061/jvs.v6i3.218/

that same program in her role as Deputy Director, National Legislative Service at the DC office of the Veterans of Foreign Wars in Washington, DC.

I wanted to know how Tammy coped with all that she has been through: her military service, the transition, and finding employment that was finally satisfying to her heart of service. She indicates that over the years it has been various therapy, medications, even avoidance of her experiences. But what is really helping propel her forward now, she says, is "being back on the water, something that I had missed so much, in a kayak or on a lake. This showed me what I can do beyond my disability." She is also now speaking up, talking with other vets, opening up about her own experiences, realizing just how much this can help her and others.

Tammy proves every day that she is resilient and empowered as she writes testimony for the record and testifies before various groups, hearings, and Congress. Her efforts not only impact the 1.5 million vets who belong to the VFW, but the 19 million vets across the country. She advocates for them all in her powerful role in the VFW Legislative Service on specific issues related to health care, mental health, suicide prevention, women veterans, minority and underserved veterans, telehealth, and caregivers.

She monitors all legislation within her portfolio and actively lobbies Congress and the Department of Veterans Affairs, interacts with members of Congress, and alerts VFW membership on legislation under discussion.

Tammy is a powerful advocate for all veterans, especially women vets. Now that I know her and have learned about her journey including the highs and the lows, I am so impressed with all she has accomplished and will do in the future. Indeed, she has come a long way since handing out basketballs and peeling chewing gum off the bleachers. You needed to hear her story in order to learn how far she has come and understand the sheer willpower and resilience she continues to display, despite all that she has gone through. As a lifetime member of the VFW, I am very pleased that she is advocating for me and all my fellow combat veterans.

CHAPTER 7

THE SISTERHOOD

Zaneta Adams

There is never a point in your career where you arrive as a woman professional. Doesn't matter what your title is or who you represent, what level you reach. People still will try to take advantage of you.

Zaneta Adams achieved what is nearly impossible: a successful career across multiple areas. As an enlisted member in all components of the Army (active duty, National Guard, and Reserves), as a mother to six children and spouse to her husband for twenty-plus years, as a successful attorney assisting veterans with compensation and pension appeals, as a founder of an organization to help women vets do much more than just survive, and finally as an appointee by the governor of Michigan to oversee all veteran affairs throughout the state. There isn't anything she cannot do. She is a powerhouse, a one-woman driving force that doesn't let anything get in her way.

Zaneta's journey to where she is today was not an easy one and is marked with physical and emotional scars; injury, pain, rehabilitation, disability, sexual assault prior to the military, and both sexual harassment and racial disparities while serving her country. The fact that she accomplished much despite adversity and trauma really goes to the determination and character of this woman.

Zaneta is a proud African American woman who was born and raised along with three siblings on the outskirts of Chicago. She moved to Florida to attend college and, since she had always had an interest in the military, she joined the Reserve Officer Training Corps (ROTC). Although she came from a family with no military service except for her great-grandmother and biological father, she joined because she wanted to help people and be of service to her country. Her parents were supportive of her decision and trusted their daughter to know what was best.

During her sophomore year, Zaneta was sexually assaulted in her own home by an individual she didn't know who had been invited over by someone else. He was not a student at the college, and it was the first time she had encountered him. Within six months of this assault, she dropped out of college and enlisted in the Army. She thought she would get some experience as an enlisted soldier, and then she could go back to ROTC to get a commission. She really wanted to learn what it was like to be enlisted before becoming an officer in charge of enlisted troops.

Of course, that is not how the military works. If you join enlisted, you are mandated to complete your term of service. There was a green to gold program for enlisted to become officers, and Zaneta figured that would be her way. "I feel like I was misled at ROTC about gaining enlisted experience and then being able to come back to school," she says. "I was young and thought I was doing the right thing. I didn't think I wouldn't be able to rejoin ROTC or go green to gold."

It wasn't quite the dream of serving as an officer that she had, but she still felt strongly about serving. She loved the values the Army espoused and believed that serving would make her a better person. While in training she met her future husband, who was also in the Army. She was all in to be all she could be, as the saying goes.

She served a total of eight years in all components of the Army: active, National Guard, and reserves. She went into the service because she wanted to feel empowered, especially after suffering a sexual assault. "I always felt like I was a strong person, and I thought if I was ever in a situation like sexual assault, I would do this, this, and this," she says. "But when you have no power in that situation, it sucks something out of you."

What was best about the military? She really enjoyed the camaraderie and the friends she made. She still keeps in touch with many she served with, and there are several that she really connected with going all the way back to basic training.

When asked what she liked least about serving, Zaneta says: "I thought I joined the Army so that I would become empowered. Ended up that I actually felt smaller in the military, was constantly being harassed, especially at basic. They picked on a lot of women and African Americans. That stands so vivid in my mind."

She was often left not really knowing why she was harassed or picked on. She frequently heard comments like, "You aren't meant to be in the military. You shouldn't even be here." She recalls: "A lot of the women were treated this way. It wasn't just African Americans. I didn't know if it was because I was a woman or because I was an African American woman." This intersectionality and conflict can bring on intense feelings that lastingly affect self-esteem, confidence, and visibility, not only while in uniform but as a veteran.

When Zaneta first joined the military, she selected 92G (cook) as her career field. She had scored very well and could have picked any field, but she chose the field she did because it had the shortest advanced training, which meant getting to serve in the *real* Army sooner. Some military occupational specialties have very long lead times before you are actually assigned to your first unit.

She remembers applying for a job as an E-3, competing against several E-6s. She got the position, but ended up angering those more senior who didn't get it. She didn't understand the politics involved, of more senior troops having an informal edge on the promotion. This made her even more of an outsider. Subsequently she couldn't get a promotion as a 92G so she ended up reclassifying to 92Y (supply), in hopes of finding positions for promotion.

This was a very isolating time for her, as she continued to be the target of harassment and the brunt of degrading comments. In 2000, she had been placed on bedrest due to pregnancy complications with her first child, and she couldn't attend training in her new career field. Zaneta indicates that she was forced to complete a urinalysis in front of observers when she was fully pregnant. She was horrified. "I didn't feel like I had a family, no sense of belonging," she says. "They were not supposed to have pregnant women do a urinalysis like that. I was embarrassed, but they just kept picking on me."

She continued to be harassed about her pregnancy and pestered with questions like, "Are you going to stay in or get out of the military now?" At one point, Zaneta and her family had bills racking up and experienced food insecurity, so her husband applied for a hardship discharge. The other men harassed him, saying things like, "We don't see why you're hurting for food. Your wife doesn't look like she is hurting for food." Zaneta was very pregnant at the time.

The degrading comments continued to mount, like, "Women should be seen not heard, and they shouldn't challenge authority." One person said to her husband in front of Zaneta, "Why can't your wife just breastfeed? Why do you need more funds for food?" She spoke up, even wrote to her senator. Her husband was told to shut her up. The gender and pregnancy discrimination she experienced was difficult to endure.

"I didn't even feel safe as a spouse because I was too mouthy, trying to get things done," Zaneta says. "They didn't like being called out by a black woman. I often tell people that I felt like I experienced more gender discrimination in the military, as it was stronger and more frequent than discrimination based on my skin color. People blatantly said women were not strong enough and shouldn't be here."

The sexual harassment was unrelenting and became more prevalent in 2005-2006, when she was attached to an infantry unit in the southern United States while undergoing training prior to deploying to Operation Iraqi Freedom. There were only ten women and 700 men. The infantry needed women to conduct gate checks of women in Iraq, so that was why women had been brought into the unit.

She recalls that she was always being asked out, receiving unwanted advances, leered at. The men didn't care that she was married; they hit on her all the time, just kept up the constant beratement. She was an Individual Ready Reserve (IRR) soldier and had been called up to attend training at several bases, in preparation for deploying to augment forces needed in Iraq.

So she didn't know any of the troops in the unit she had been attached to, neither the few women nor the many men. "I walked into the unit and felt so uncomfortable, all males, I felt all eyes on me and looking at me as if I was a piece of meat, a piece of meat being thrown to the wolves."

Zaneta kept getting offers to go out but continued to decline, pointing out that she was married. Since she wouldn't go out with any of the guys, vicious rumors started that she was gay. "I was terribly offended by this. I was married, had a husband. But they didn't care, it was nonstop." She remembers saying so many times that she was not interested, all to no avail. Several of the men just kept up the unwanted advances, some of them even telling her they could imagine what she looked like under the uniform. It was unrelenting, she felt isolated, alone and in a constant state of hypervigilance.

The daily harassment was exhausting and hard to withstand. A couple of male sergeants acted as battle buddies for her, and she trusted them to help keep her safe. But the sexual harassment, inappropriate sexualized comments, gender slurs, leering, and come-ons took its toll. It was also difficult that her husband didn't really understand the extreme harassment and the climate she was in. At times he questioned her fidelity, which hurt her deeply. Zaneta reveals that her experience being one of only a few women among so many men affected their marriage when she returned home, and to some extent still does. She says she is assertive, but when it comes to sexual assault and sexual harassment, it is very hard to be assertive, because she didn't feel properly prepared or trained to handle these situations.

Even today, in her position leading all veteran services for the state of Michigan, at an event recently she encountered inappropriate comments. "I just froze, couldn't say anything." Quite possibly this incident brought up her previous experiences and trauma.

Zaneta says with feeling that she believes women cannot escape the deep and intense feelings surrounding this type of trauma. "There is never a point in your career where you arrive as a woman professional," she says. "Doesn't matter what your title is or who you represent, what level you reach. People still will try to take advantage of you."

While undergoing combat training prior to deploying to Iraq, she was in an accident that left her with permanent injuries, resulting in a painful and lengthy rehabilitation. She was severely injured during a combat simulation, performing a rapid dismount in full combat gear from a deuce and a half truck with the rails up. She fell approximately eleven feet, crushing several discs in her lower back.

Incredibly, the unit still wanted to deploy her to Iraq. It was only during the final signoff that a physician really listened to her describe her injuries and pain and ordered imagery. Immediately upon seeing the results of the MRI, he declared her nondeployable. She endured two back surgeries.

Medically separated in 2006 after eleven long months of a protracted and extremely complex medical evaluation board process, she was not returned to duty and was medically discharged with 20 percent disability. This low level meant that she would not receive full benefits. She never gave up on the uphill battle to get appropriate disability and compensation. Finally, in 2008, the Department of Veterans Affairs (VA) completed a review and indicated that Zaneta should be at 100 percent disability. The Army then retroactively upgraded her initial assessment of 20 percent to 50 percent. Her medical retirement became official in 2018, thirteen years after suffering her injury. Navigating benefits from the military and the VA is a daunting process, not for the faint of heart. The fact that she ultimately prevailed speaks directly to her perseverance and determination.

After this entire episode and years of fighting, Zaneta didn't stop with her own case. She decided to go back to school to complete her bachelor's degree and then go on to law school. She wanted to be in a position to help her fellow vets with their legal struggles surrounding benefits they had earned. She had a new mission and felt that calling strongly.

Immediately after leaving the military, and still dealing with her injury, she fell into a deep depression. She says she didn't do much, but this is hard to believe as she had six kids, including two sets of twins. "Women don't get that downtime," she reflects. "I was having trouble ambulating, but it was kind of like, okay, you're back, get back to the business of being a mom. I didn't really have any time for self-care."

Compounding her rehabilitation and caring for her children was the difficulty in reacclimating to the household and just being a mom again. She had spent almost a year away from her family in the military. Her husband had managed everything while she was gone, and he had done a good job of running the household and taking care of the kids. The family had picked up the pieces while she was gone, and reintegration of Mom was going to take adjustment on everyone's part. Her kids would often ask her husband, "When is Mommy leaving again? When are we taking her to the airport?"

In the fall of 2006, Zaneta went back to civilian employment. But she found that she couldn't sit for very long. Her back was quite painful. Following up with a physician, she found out that she had a tumor, a hematoma on her nerve, which stemmed from the accident to her spine in 2005. She needed surgery, as the tumor was inside the nerve, so the nerve needed to be severed in her lower back. Zaneta recalls that she couldn't sit before the surgery and unfortunately ended up worse after it.

"I felt like I was betrayed," she says. "The Army should have found the tumor way back when I had my first surgery after falling." Her second surgery left her with loss of feeling. She can still feel pressure, but not really the pain in her leg. As a disabled veteran, Zaneta's physical healing continues to be a long journey, with good days and bad days.

While attending Cooley Law School at Western Michigan University, she used a cane as she progressed in her rehabilitation. Although not the top academically, she was very active and engaged, graduating in 2014 as one of two distinguished law students. Following graduation she worked for a law firm in Michigan. It was there that she began to fulfill her dream of helping veterans with compensation and pension appeals while also immersing herself in municipal law, contract law, civil law, and prosecutions. Who better to help vets than a vet herself, who had gone through the complexities of fighting and traversing the military and veteran government bureaucracies? She related to her clients all too well.

Achieving success as an attorney helping others might have been enough for the average person, but Zaneta wanted to do more. She became an advocate and spokesperson for Challenge America, a national veteran resource organization. Zaneta believes strongly in the work this nonprofit does and remembers how genuine they were. They motivated her and helped her gain the courage to do even more. The catalyst for jumpstarting her own healing from trauma was a gathering she attended for women vets in Aspen, Colorado in 2009, where many came together and shared their experiences.

These events tailored to women vets were outstanding but were typically held once a year. Zaneta knew that more frequent programming was needed. She stepped in to fill the void, creating WINC: For All Women Veterans (Women Injured in Combat).

WINC is an advocacy organization for women active duty and veterans. Zaneta is the founder, served as the group's first president, and later moved into an advisory role. "I felt that all of us have had some type of injury," she says, "whether it be physical, mental, moral, spiritual, or emotional, while serving in the military, whether any of us care to admit it or not. So I decided to create WINC for women vets."

Basically, Zaneta wanted to honor women vets and encourage, revive, and restore them with meetups, retreats, peer support groups, and MST events all across the country. Then in 2017 she established the Military Sisterhood Initiative, a national peer support network, in conjunction with WINC. Zaneta partnered with Challenge America for the initiative, resulting in a network of more than 5,000 women from all over the world.

I wrote a poem titled "The Sisterhood" not long after Zaneta and I met. My poem was in response to an event I attended at the Military Women's Memorial. Surrounded by so many women vets from all eras and services in a safe place, to openly share our experiences, inspired me. The event also really drove home for me just how powerful Zaneta's work with women vets really is. In the first lines of "The Sisterhood," I share her passion regarding the strong bonds we have as women vets.

I am a woman veteran, part of an awesome Sisterhood
that is very much alive and well,
diverse and prospering with every lived experience shared

Diagnosed with PTSD, Zaneta's healing journey consists of various therapies and approaches, including years of cognitive processing therapy and more recently Cereset, a non-invasive process using sound to relax the brain, allowing it to reset itself. The physical pain, especially the nerve pain she endures daily, contributes to the anxiety she feels. "A lot of my anxiety comes from my pain, as I don't know when it will come or if it will hit me really hard," she told me. "I struggled with it for years and now understand that treating my PTSD can help my overall health." Importantly, her efforts with WINC and the sisterhood initiative continue to provide engagement with women vets, furthering her own healing.

She left her law firm and the leadership of WINC in 2019, as she was offered another dream job: as the director, appointed by the governor, of MVAA, the Veterans Affairs Agency of the entire state of Michigan. Zaneta is the first woman and person of color, and the first woman veteran cabinet member in the state of Michigan. This is where one finds her today, shaping Michigan's support of veterans. According to the MVAA website, the agency "works to identify and break down barriers veterans face in employment, education, health care and quality of life to make Michigan a great place for veterans and their families to call home." Zaneta continues to impact veterans in many positive ways, always advocating for them in all her roles.

Zaneta was recognized recently with the 2021 Lakeshore Innovator of the Year Award by Grand Valley's Muskegon Innovation Hub. This was due to her work with WINC, the Military Sisterhood Initiative, and her many efforts to assist women vets and to assist in lowering the rate of veteran suicide. Additionally, in 2021 she was honored as a Department of Veterans Affairs Trailblazer and appointed to the new Department of Veterans Affairs working group for sexual assault and harassment prevention. Finally, she was the powerhouse behind Michigan's women veteran recognition day, held in June each year throughout the state.

Zaneta has come a long way from a young private first class in the Army. She proves every day that she is unstoppable, never satisfied with the status quo, always looking to improve everything she touches, and she hasn't allowed previous traumas, both physical and emotional, to define her or stop her from pursuing her mission. Her lived experiences prove that one can truly do it all, albeit with the visible scars and invisible wounds of true service and sacrifice. Her wounds do not define her, have never prevented her from that inner drive to make a real difference in the lives of veterans. She has touched thousands of women vets. I am so proud to call her my sister.

CHAPTER 8

ACTIONS NOT WORDS

K. Denise Rucker Krepp

People are given a voice for a reason, and they need to use their voice so people can hear and learn about sexual assault and sexual harassment. It is important for passionate people to continue taking up this fight. Absent our voices, our noise, this just keeps occurring.

Denise Krepp is a Coast Guard veteran, an attorney, someone who has experienced forms of sexual harassment firsthand and assisted others who have been sexually assaulted. She is a former political appointee who was asked to resign because she sought an investigation into sexual assault and sexual harassment at the U.S. Merchant Marine Academy, a local elected official in Washington, DC, and the DC Ambassador for the Military Women's Memorial. And these are just a few of Denise's many roles. Grass doesn't grow long under her feet. She is a mover and shaker, hellbent on getting stuff done.

Denise says she has been a member of the sexual assault support community going back thirty years. She became a trained rape counselor and has been able to help many, starting with her experiences in law school before she joined the military, while serving, and to this day.

After attending The George Washington University, Denise attended law school in Florida. Although she had a good experience with the academic rigors of law school, it was there that she experienced her first incident of sexual harassment and where a fellow student was raped.

Denise was sexually harassed verbally by a male fellow law student, the typical misogynistic comments and objectification of women. She heard her body described in a degrading manner and had sexually explicit lewd remarks aimed at her. But she decided not to tolerate such degrading, offensive comments and reported the incident to the dean of the law school, asking him to address the issue. Denise says she was disappointed when the dean failed to properly address the complaint.

Compounding the issue was the reaction from some of her fellow women law students. They asked her why she was making such a big deal of the incident. Denise was dumbfounded. She had been harassed, and she had trusted in the system enough to report the incident, then absolutely nothing had happened. The harasser was not dealt with in any formal manner by the leadership of the law school. These were law students, learning about the law and the equitable treatment of their fellow citizens, and yet one of their own was not held accountable to some of the very laws they were being taught. The failure of leadership to address issues of sexual harassment could potentially have lifelong considerations for those in the wake of the harasser's actions and for those who could be targeted in the future. The harasser was allowed to continue with no admonishment and graduated.

Several of Denise's fellow law students knew that this type of behavior should not be allowed to stand. Let's just say that the situation was dealt with in a very informal way; Denise's friends demonstratively showed him the error of his ways. He never bothered Denise again.

Another incident occurred when one of her friends, a student at the university, was raped. Denise recognized in the woman's behavior the symptoms that she had learned about in sexual assault victims. She knew something had changed; she could see the signs. She asked her friend if she had been raped. Her friend said yes, by a student at the university. Her friend was so distraught at both what had happened to her and how she had been treated after the rape. She had been asked not to say anything and not to report it.

Denise asked her friend if anyone at the university had helped her, and no one had so Denise spoke with her and helped her as best she could. This case was so very sad in many ways. Beyond the horrific rape, no one seemed to care for the victim. All these years later, this incident has stayed with Denise, and it still drives her to speak with young women in college to this day. It also became a strong motivating element for her advocacy and activism against sexual assault.

One could say that these incidents prepared Denise for what she would soon experience in the military. After all, it was 1998 and throughout the armed forces there was a culture that allowed sexism, misogyny, and harassment to exist and at times thrive.

Denise's family was deeply rooted in service to the country. Both her parents had served as officers in the Army. Her father attended West Point, was a Ranger, and saw combat in Vietnam. Her mother came from a Navy family and got her own commission in the Army through Officer Candidate School. Denise had grown up in the Army. Born in Atlanta, she had attended high school in Germany and lived all over the world. The nomadic military life was in this family's blood.

So when Denise informed her family that she was going into the Coast Guard, her parents didn't wonder about her serving, but they did wonder why she wasn't going Army. Denise says she became a coastie because she "thought it would be a cool job." She thought her fellow law students were going to end up in white shoe law firms, and what could be cooler than a mission focused on guns, drugs, and immigrants. To young Denise that sounded exciting, far from a boring attorney job.

She joined the Coast Guard under the direct commissioning program, since she already had her college and law degrees. She attended Direct Commissioning Officer School in Yorktown, Virginia and became what was commonly referred to as a thirty-day wonder. This was a short, direct route to serving as a commissioned officer in the Coast Guard. The school has since moved to the academy; Denise's class was the last one conducted at Yorktown, where a lot of other training schools are co-located.

At Yorktown, her commissioning cohort had thirty men and four women.

She heard sexist remarks such as, "The only reason you're in this direct commission program is because you're a female." Some people questioned her progress and attributed it not to her ability or merit but to the fact that she was a woman. Comments similar to these were frequent during her four years as a coastie.

Her father and a Ranger buddy attended her graduation. He looked around and said, "What is this?" Direct commissioning as an attorney into the military was indeed different from most standard commission programs.

It is important to note that the Coast Guard is the only military service not under the Department of Defense (DoD). Prior to September 11, 2001 the Coast Guard fell under the Department of Transportation, but it was moved under the newly created Department of Homeland Security in 2003. It is both a federal law enforcement agency and a military force. According to the Coast Guard itself: "In times of peace, it operates as part of the Department of Homeland Security enforcing the nation's laws at sea, protecting the marine environment, guarding the nation's vast coastline and ports, and performing vital lifesaving missions. In times of war, or at the direction of the President, the Coast Guard serves under the Department of the Navy, defending the nation against terrorism and foreign threats."[1]

Denise served four years and was stationed at Coast Guard headquarters for all four years. Prior to 9/11 she worked in legislative affairs, where she reviewed and wrote legislation. After 9/11 she served as primary counsel for surface and maritime security matters, and in this role she helped create the Department of Homeland Security. "I was literally in the room when the maritime environment was being created post 9/11," she says. She was part of, and witnessed, sweeping structural changes to our country's national defense apparatus.

But it wasn't always easy for her at the Coast Guard headquarters. It can be a tough assignment for any young officer right out of training, made even more difficult if you were a young woman officer in the late 1990s. "The culture at the headquarters was one that treated young women like red meat," remembers Denise. Women were treated inappropriately simply

---

1 https://www.gocoastguard.com

for being women. Sexual harassment was commonplace, and women were viewed from a predatory standpoint.

Intensifying this environment was the fact that there were no women admirals or other senior officers. "There was no one I could aspire to be, no one for me to look up to." Yet Denise stood out. She tried to just do her job and carried herself in a confident manner. Since she had grown up in the military, she knew she had to play the game. She believes that her experiences previously as an athlete and growing up in the military helped her have confidence in her own ability to succeed and to handle herself. When I asked if she felt welcome, safe, or comfortable while she served, Denise's response was illuminating: "There is a difference between feeling safe and believing in one's own ability to handle things."

"I got used to being the only woman in the room," she told me. She knew she was being watched and that any mistakes she made would reflect not only on her. Weighing heavily on her was knowing that whatever she did in any situation would reflect on all the women who served after her.

It helped tremendously that Denise is quite tall, at five feet ten inches. When she wore heels, she was easily over six feet. She towered over most of the men and deliberately wore heels. And it worked, most of the time. It seemed to work well when she traveled to Cartagena, Colombia as part of a drug interdiction operation. She was one of few women there, surrounded by men, and it was a dangerous time to be in Colombia. But the guys there had her back, although they were more impressed with her ability to speak Spanish than with the fact that she was an attorney. She helped them negotiate prices and buy things for their families.

On one occasion Denise was asked out. This was nothing new, occurred all the time, she was constantly being hit on. But what was different about this time, was that it was by a Colombian officer. She agreed to go out to dinner, didn't really think much about it, until he showed up in a private boat. The guys in her group told her: No way are you getting on that boat. Her captain even spoke out very clearly: "Do not go." She wholeheartedly agreed. She realized that it had been a very bad idea to agree to go to dinner with him. The rebels were just thirty miles from the city. Who knows what might have happened if she had gone? She might never have been heard from again.

Denise recalls that the first boss she had was a true professional, mentored her and helped her gain experience so she could have some street cred. But, she says, the second one retaliated against her after she reported irregularities with the safeguarding of classified material in the office. Keeping classified material safe is a serious issue, and one of her adjunct duties as a Classified Material Control Officer was to assess the unit for vulnerabilities. They were not in a SCIF (sensitive compartmented information facility), and there was a foreign national working there. She sought outside help, filed a report about the assessment, and brought attention to the command.

She was asked to drop the request for assistance, or she would be retaliated against in her annual evaluation. Her boss clearly verbalized what would happen to her if she didn't do as asked. So she very clearly said no and stood her ground. Her evaluation was indeed marked down. Denise believes firmly that this retaliation in the form of a lower annual evaluation would not have happened if she had been a male.

There were incidents when the harassing, sexist comments came directly from senior officers, and her height advantage didn't work all that well. Denise remembers that, when she was a young lieutenant, a senior officer at headquarters kept hitting on her. Whenever she met with him, she would make sure to ask about his wife and children. She was relentless in this, waging a one-woman battle, reminding him of all the women and girls in his life. After a time, he stopped hitting on her.

There was an incident involving another woman at the headquarters that Denise remembers well. The officers gossiped, openly and in salacious, lurid detail, about this woman's background and sexual activities. Denise recalls it as absolutely disgusting to observe. She had never ever seen people gossip like that, certainly had never seen this behavior occur about the men's sexual activities. It was totally unprofessional and inappropriate.

By this time, Denise had seen enough sexism and misconduct that she knew what it would be like if she stayed in. "I didn't want to be retaliated against my entire career," she says. "Plus, I wasn't an academy graduate, and I was female. The odds of making captain [O-6] were just not good."

Another important factor was that it was now 2002 and she had married a naval surface warfare officer the year prior. "I realized that one of us needed to get out," she told me. "Life was about to get very difficult, with both of us serving on active duty during wartime."

Denise worked various jobs after leaving the Coast Guard. One of them was as the Maritime Administration's Chief Counsel. It was in this role that she would once again experience retaliation, this time on a grander scale. Denise says that she had been appointed into this role as a political appointee and was forced to resign due to her request for an Inspector General investigation into widespread sexual assault and sexual harassment at the Merchant Marine Academy.

She had been notified that there was sexual assault and sexual harassment going on at the academy and at sea. Not just student on student, but professor on student as well. And it involved all classifications of students, women and men, from freshmen to seniors. Once she was able to corroborate the information through speaking with multiple parties and by receiving a letter from a whistleblower, she went up through her chain of command, requesting a full Inspector General investigation at the Department of Transportation level.

According to Denise, the then Secretary of Transportation, who at the time oversaw the Maritime Administration, informed the general counsel to have the IG stand down and not to conduct an investigation. Absolutely nothing happened; the issue was buried. No one helped the survivors; no policies were enacted. In fact, the survivors refused to speak up. They were very scared of retaliation from leadership, especially when they saw what happened to Denise for trying to get the investigation started. Denise was asked to either resign or be fired. She chose to resign. She was told that she was being removed for lack of confidence in her leadership. Denise believes that in essence she was forcibly fired for standing up and requesting an investigation into sexual assault and sexual harassment at the academy.

What makes this entire situation so sad is that just a few years later, in 2016, the academy had a stand down linked to sexual assault. That same year, the academy's sea year program was discontinued due to allegations of sexual assaults. It has since been reinstated, and in 2021 allegations of sea year sexual assaults resurfaced in a big way. How many more men and women have been harassed or assaulted due to inaction all those years ago? Denise brought up the issue but was completely shut down and pushed out.

But no one can shut down her voice. She continues to speak up about the leadership failures at the academy and the retaliation she received for coming to the aid of sexual assault victims. Denise states passionately: "People are given a voice for a reason, and they need to use their voice so people can hear and learn about sexual assault and sexual harassment. It is important for passionate people to continue taking up this fight. Absent our voices, our noise, this just keeps occurring."

Denise is a prolific writer and has written several opinion pieces about sexual harassment and sexual assault. In 2013 she wrote a piece titled "Female Military Personnel Aren't Whores," after she witnessed a female midshipman being asked in a military hearing whether she was a whore, how she performed oral sex, and whether she had on undergarments when she attended a particular party. This type of questioning was inexcusable, and Denise clearly said so.

In 2014, Denise provided testimony before the Response Systems Panel on Military Sexual Assault. She testified about her forced resignation and recommended changes in the processes that address MST, military sexual trauma. Also in 2014 she published a powerful opinion piece in *The Maritime Executive* titled "Combatting Sexual Assault in the Military, in which she stated something quite profound: "Military Sexual Assault is a domestic enemy. It inhibits good order and discipline and is a threat that must be destroyed." [2] Why has it taken years for people to acknowledge this?

In 2017 Denise presented at her alma mater, the Elliot School of International Affairs at The George Washington University, as part of an Why Ethics Matter speaker series. The title of her remarks was "Sexual Assault at

---

2 Published February 3, 2014. Online at https://www.maritime-executive.com/features/MarEx-OPED-Combatting-Sexual-Assault-in-the-Military-2014-02-03.

a Federal Service Academy, a Whistleblower's Perspective." She spoke about what occurred at the Merchant Marine Academy and her resignation, and provided advice to help survivors and advocates.

In 2019, she testified before the Civil Rights Commission, again asking that the leadership be held accountable for "failing to act, for creating hostile living conditions for Congressionally nominated young men and women attending the federal service school." Much of what Denise spoke about continues to occur. When will change finally happen? In 2021 there was a move within the DoD to take sexual assault and sexual harassment out of the chain of command. Congress has been applying much needed pressure; however, this would be within DoD, and the Coast Guard falls under the Department of Homeland Security. Denise is adamant that what is occurring in DoD regarding this issue must also occur within the Coast Guard.

Denise is a one-woman powerhouse trying to make a difference. She is using her platform and practices what she preaches about change, using both actions and words and demanding accountability from others. "The only way to affect change is to use your voice," she says.

How does she cope with everything she has gone through and continues to be involved in? Denise speaks up and writes about the issues important to her. She also uses gardening to decompress. She said to me: "Go kill a weed". Denise wisely says that if gardening is not for you, find something that you can do. We all need outlets to help us, because speaking out and advocating for change are quite stressful.

She spends time with her family. She loves to write about successful women who served in the Navy and about minority women. "I've learned that the person who controls the pen controls what's out there," she asserts. Well said, Denise. I am proud to know you and to advocate alongside you on the issues we're both passionate about. Our combined voices can have an impact.

CHAPTER 9

SEMPER FI

Stesha Colby-Lynch

We started sharing our stories and why we never reported our sexual harassment and sexual assault. We found out that we all had the same abusers at the same time as one another, but the culture of machismo made it so we couldn't even trust fellow women.

Stesha Colby-Lynch joined the Marines because, to her at age twenty-one, it just seemed like they were the toughest branch in the armed forces and if she went into the Corps, she wouldn't be messed with. How wrong she turned out to be.

Five and a half months into her service as a Marine, she was sexually assaulted in a training environment. Stesha also experienced sexual harassment and would go on to be sexually assaulted two more times during her four-year enlistment.

Although she made some great bonds and friendships during her time in service, her enlistment was marred by the few predators among her many brothers. Their betrayal would stay with her for years and continue to impact her life as she moved forward after leaving military service.

Stesha grew up in the Dallas-Fort Worth metroplex. Her family relocated to Memphis, Tennessee when she was in eighth grade. That was quite a shock for her. "I had a different accent," she says. "It was an inner-city school in a heavily gang area, and the kids there were tough. I was the short, tiny, quiet, nerdy kid who made good grades." Of course, being smart didn't win her any favors from the other kids.

Stesha describes that school environment as being the worst. She was constantly getting picked on, and kids would throw things at her. She says that she was too short and nerdy to be a jock, so she became the manager for the girls' basketball team in the hopes she could fit in. Stesha remembers being the only white kid on her school bus and that one time another student, a boy, reached around the seats to grab her breasts.

She told her parents about the incident, and they made her tell the boy's parents. They were apologetic and surprised at their son's behavior. Things just got worse on the bus and at school, as she became known as a rat.

Trying again to fit in, she became the statistician for the boys' baseball team and found sort of a home there. She was treated well by the players and supporters. She enjoyed being part of the team and her yearning to fit in just might have been a precursor to her serving, putting a team and its mission first.

Her family ended up moving to a better school district in the suburbs. The first week there, Stesha got in trouble for fighting. She stood up to a bully who was calling a younger student homophobic slurs. She was rewarded by being suspended.

After high school Stesha wanted to join the military, but her mother persuaded her to go to college and told her she could always join after college as an officer. So Stesha went to college in Tennessee, even though she had no idea what she wanted to do with her life, much less what to major in. She says her parents expected her to know what she wanted to do with her life, but at this point in her young life, she had no idea what she wanted to do. She ended up changing her major four times.

"I knew I wasn't emotionally ready for college, but I did what my parents wanted like a good little 18-year-old does," Stesha remembers. No surprise then when she dropped out at 19 and followed a guy she had been dating to Louisiana. He was in the Air Force and had been assigned to Barksdale AFB.

Looking back, Stesha acknowledges that she had latched on to this Air

Force guy as a way to get away from home, school, and her indecisive life. "I had this epiphany," she says. "I was like, Do I really want to escape my life the way my mom did, by getting married young and having babies? The answer to that was definitely no." So she told her boyfriend that she was going back home to Memphis, but she really went back to college.

Stesha says that she had been back in college for a semester when her roommate was raped. She had gone to a party with her boyfriend, but stayed on after her boyfriend departed. Another student offered her a ride home, and he raped her in his car.

The events that followed that incident remain indelible in Stesha's mind to this day. Stesha helped her roommate contact campus police to report the assault and was appalled at the response. According to Stesha the campus police said, "Well, you got in his car, and it's basically a 'He said, she said' issue." She was livid, so she struck out on her own to do something about it.

Stesha took a baseball bat, found the alleged perpetrator's car, and "just went to town on it," she says. "I was so mad that I didn't think about the consequences, that I could get arrested. I was vandalizing a brand new 2005 BMW." She went back to her dorm room thinking the police would be on their way soon to arrest her. But nothing ever happened. Stesha recalls finding out later that this particular individual had had previous incidents and apparently been transferred to many schools. She says that his father pulled him out of school and moved him yet again. The injustice was never lost on her.

It was quite a shock to her when, just two weeks later, Stesha herself was raped by a fellow student, an Army vet. Stesha met him in one of her classes, and he invited her to a campus party. She went with him and drank heavily. In fact, she doesn't remember leaving the party and going to her place. She woke when her roommate was banging on the front door. The vet had double bolted the door.

As she came to, she recalls she was naked and felt the vet on top of her having sex. And not really sex, but rape, Stesha says, as she had been totally out. She states adamantly that at no time did she give consent for him to do what he did. He jumped off her and hightailed it out of the dorm, stepping on and breaking her laptop as he ran out. She was devastated and wonders how much further could it have gone if her roommate had not arrived when she did.

Compounding the assault was the fact that she couldn't even report it, as she knew exactly what the police would say: "Well, you went out with him, and you drank too much." She had seen the total lack of concern and empathy for what had happened to her roommate just two weeks prior.

Stesha began to shut down, no longer attending classes, trying to avoid her perpetrator, and losing touch with all her friends. One day, she was sitting in the dining hall on campus and the man who had raped her sat down across from her. She told one of her friends what had happened, and they questioned whether it had really happened. She couldn't believe that one of her supposed friends could even say that. After this, she shut down completely.

The trauma left her feeling anxious, isolated, and scared. Her grades understandably dropped, and she was placed on academic probation and dismissal. She knew that if she got kicked out of school, she had to get a Plan B. No way would her parents tolerate her quitting school without a plan. Ironically while sitting in a common area of the university reading the letter dismissing her from school, she looked up and saw a poster for the Marines. She thought to herself, "Now that would be my Plan B."

Knowing that her parents would want her to thoroughly check out options, she approached a recruiting station where she could speak with all the services. "The Air Force said 'No, because you used pot in the past,' and they wouldn't waive it," she recalls. "The Army said they didn't have jobs for linguists, which is what I wanted; they wanted me to go open contract. It was 2005, and the Army just needed bodies. The Navy said they didn't allow women on their ships, which was not true but is what they told me. The Marines said, 'Sure, we'll take you, as long as you don't do drugs on active duty.'"

Stesha got the job she wanted, but she had to wait six months before going to basic, as she had to lose weight and get within the standards. She thought to herself, "Marines are the toughest branch, so at least I won't get fucked with." After what had happened to her in college, she welcomed the Marine family and was ready to be a tough Marine.

Stesha knew she was going to be a linguist, but didn't know what language she would be assigned. She wanted Russian but was given Arabic, an extremely difficult language to learn. This would mean a two-year-long school at the Defense Language Institute in Monterey, California. She walked into what seemed a paradise setting: an oceanside base in a resort town. What could go wrong?

Sexual harassment was common. Stesha remembers that being a woman surrounded by so many men was tough, and that the dynamics on base were aggressive. "You had to act aggressive like the men, drink as hard as they did, cuss, tell dirty jokes, laugh at dirty jokes," she recalls. "If you weren't aggressive, you got left behind."

And Stesha didn't want to be left behind. What she had going for her was that her fellow student linguists were as nerdy as she was. They were men, but they were like her, fellow geeks going to school for language.

She remembers a drill instructor telling her in basic training, "You all need to be careful. This will be the last time you will be around this many women. You're going into the fleet or school, and guys are going to say one or two things about you, they will try to sleep with you, they'll be knocking on your door. If you don't sleep with them, they're going to say you're a lesbian. And if you do sleep with them, they'll say you're a whore. It's a lose-lose situation, so protect yourself. Prepare yourselves." This was probably some of the best advice she received from another woman and fellow Marine.

But Stesha believed she could handle the guys, and she let her guard down. After all, these guys were like her, and she felt part of the Marine family.

That safe and secure feeling totally fell apart within her first month in language school in Monterey. Stesha says she was raped by a fellow student in linguist training, a sailor. She met him at a bar. He told her that he had seen her around at the chow hall and really liked how vivacious she was. She was known for her raunchy jokes and outgoing personality. "I don't know if he saw that about me and wanted to break it or what," she says.

He was good-looking and really smart. So when he hit on her and started buying her drinks, she wasn't concerned, as he was a fellow linguist. She remembers leaving the bar with him, allowing him to walk her home. She woke up the next morning sore in places that she shouldn't be and had no recollection of anything beyond starting to walk home.

When she went to the chow hall that next morning, she was greeted by puzzling comments: "Thanks for the show. Great show." What show? She had no idea what they were referring to. It wasn't until two months later, when she ran into a different sailor in town, that she found out what had happened that night.

This is what Stesha could piece together from her own disjointed memories and the sailor's comments: While walking back to the barracks after drinking at the bar with the linguist, she must have passed out. Then he raped her in the woods in front of his barracks. The guys who watched from the barracks didn't know that she was passed out. This was the show the guys had been congratulating her on. She was completely horrified. She had been raped in front of the barracks, and no one had done anything to help her. The sailor who told her what he had witnessed admitted that he didn't know she was passed out.

It had been over a year since her sexual assault in college. She had worked so hard to become stronger, and now around her brothers and sisters in the Marines, thinking she was safe, she had let her guard down. "Everything in boot camp prepared me for the wolf to be at the door," she says. "But nothing prepared me for the wolf to be already in the house."

Life was never the same. This first sexual assault on active duty totally blindsided her. She still had some good people around her, who supported her and in whom she could confide – though not necessarily about the sexual assault – but she couldn't get past the betrayal that had occurred. "After this incident, I never felt safe again while I served in the military," she asserts.

Soon after this assault, she became involved in a toxic relationship with a fellow Marine. Stesha continually excused his bad behavior. According to her, they would go out to dinner, and he would ply her with alcohol even when she said she didn't want any more. She would tell him she wanted to go home to the barracks but would find herself in a hotel with him after waking up sore and unsure how she got there. He would get her blackout drunk and have sex with her without her consent. She wondered whether he might have drugged her drinks.

Finally, after one disastrous episode when her parents were visiting, she was able to break it off with him. Stesha says he actually urinated on an officer's car in front of her parents. That finally shocked her into reality. Stesha wonders if her previous sexual assault had been related in any way to her getting involved in this very toxic relationship. She now finds it hard to believe that she allowed herself to be abused in that way. Strangely, after she broke it off, this Marine told others that she was the aggressor, that she would get him drunk and take advantage of him.

She found herself isolated again, with no one really believing her except for her roommate, or so she thought. Years later she found out that she was indeed believed, but that no one spoke out about it at the time.

Slowly, she tried to get out of the depression she was in and started to hang out with her roommate's friends. It was among them that she found a boyfriend, another Marine who treated her with respect and was an overall great guy. She began to trust again, to open up and let down her guard. She had a good group that she felt were like family to her.

The group looked out for each other and helped transition new linguist students to school. A new student arrived that kind of creeped everyone out. They called him the creep, and Stesha remembers telling her friends not to be alone with him. One day Stesha went to their neighborhood bar that catered to veterans and military, along with friends and her boyfriend. Everything was going fine – until she went to change the music in the jukebox.

The new student, a Marine linguist, followed her and while Stesha's boyfriend was playing darts with his back to them, she says this creepy fellow Marine tried to kiss her and groped her breasts. Stesha was totally shocked. The nerve of this guy, to assault her while her boyfriend was right there. She did what came automatically to her: She punched him in the throat. The bartender witnessed the incident, and so did her boyfriend's best friend, but not her boyfriend. The bartender acted quickly and had the bouncer evict him from the premises. Stesha never told her boyfriend; she knew he would go after him.

Instead, she and her boyfriend's best friend paid him a visit and informed him that he was out of their social group and if they ever saw him in their bar, they would report him. They all knew that the incident, combined with the drinking, would get him kicked out of school. "I should have reported it and not just threatened to do so," Stesha says now. She started to doubt herself: "What mixed signals did I give, that let him think that this was okay?" She began to internalize the whole situation, and it ate her up.

Years later, Stesha heard that this same Marine had gone on to assault other Marines. She regrets not reporting the incident and still has guilt to this day. It has only been through therapy that she has been able to see that what occurred was not her fault, and that she did the right thing for herself at that time, in that situation. Further realizations were unearthed after the murder of Vanessa Guillén.

Stesha began to speak with women that she served with, and they finally opened up to each other about their experiences with military sexual trauma. "We started sharing our stories and why we never reported our sexual harassment and sexual assault," she says. "We found out that we all had the same abusers at the same time as one another, but the culture of machismo made it so we couldn't even trust fellow women. Two of us were sexually assaulted by the same sailor weeks apart from one another, and we never knew – and we were pretty close and remain close today. So many conversations, and so many negative feelings and repressed memories have arisen due to Vanessa's murder."

After two years at DLI, Stesha completed Arabic language training and received both college credit and a certificate. But she did not pass the Marines proficiency test for Arabic, so she was reclassified into Administration. She attended Admin school then was assigned to Joint Reserve Base Carswell in Fort Worth, Texas.

The joint base was actually a reserve Air Force base, and she was the only active-duty lower enlisted Marine there. Immediately after arriving, she was met with sexual harassment. Stesha says that one of the officers in charge, a reserve captain, told her that women should not be in the Corps. She was met with overt hostility from the minute she arrived.

Stesha also was harassed about her height and weight. She would go to the gym and work out furiously. In fact, she developed an eating disorder. It wasn't anorexia or bulimia, but she would starve herself and work out hardcore, doing physical training three times a day. Others would see her at the gym and inform the leadership that Stesha was really kicking butt working out.

She recalls that, instead of saying that her dedication and working out were admirable, some of the leadership would say to others: "Then why is she still so fucking fat?" She was required to be taped weekly. "I am gifted with a larger chest," Stesha says, "and at 5'2", my physique just didn't bode well for Marine standards." It was a constant battle for her and she became depressed, always on edge, terrified of being kicked out due to weight. With each passing day she became more isolated.

She lived in the barracks with the other geographic bachelors, but she didn't have any peers on the base. Everyone her age was an officer or NCO. "People avoided me because of who I was and where I worked, the legal office," she says. She turned to alcohol and people from other branches. She had no Marine friends at this unit.

Alcohol was just one of several inappropriate coping mechanisms that Stesha used throughout her military service. She also smoked heavily, up to a pack and a half a day. She isolated herself, shut down, and never really talked openly about what she was going through, but she never sought therapy while on active duty. "It was beaten into us that if we had to take meds for anything, we would get kicked out," she says. One of her friends sought help and was medically boarded out of the military.

Stesha married a few years ago and is happy living a more authentic life. Since she left the service in 2010, she has tried talk therapy, EMDR, writing, reconnecting and speaking honestly with those she served with – both men and women – getting in touch with nature, and hiking with her husband and dogs. "Nature has always been my go-to Zen space," she says. "Hiking until you're exhausted is so much healthier than drinking until you forget." On the day we met up for our first interview, Stesha had completed a seven-mile hike. She definitely is working on her wellbeing, both mental and physical.

She completed her bachelor's degree from Texas Christian University and went on to work for the Texas Veterans Commission as an education co-ordinator. In 2021 she and her husband decided to take a huge leap of faith and travel the country writing and working in their new business, a pet adventure company offering more than the traditional pet care services, called Pawsitive Adventures. Stesha loves animals and brought her dog Hercules with her to visit with me. It took a lot of courage for her to leave the traditional workforce and a steady paycheck to start her own business and travel the country, but she is loving it and happy. Stesha is working on a memoir of her life and experiences in the military.

Interestingly, and sadly, it was after my op-ed about my own sexual assault and sexual harassment was published that Stesha reached out to me.[1] We had known each other for a few years and had collaborated on events in higher education for veterans, but we had not known that we were both MST survivors. Only after my op-ed was published in November 2020, following the murder of Vanessa Guillén, did we begin sharing stories. Stesha continues to help me on my own healing journey. She and so many others reassure me that I am not alone.

Stesha's story is not an easy one to tell, for she has suffered greatly. Enduring a sexual assault before the military, and additional assaults while on active duty, along with various forms of harassment, is almost too much for one person to bear. But she still stands, exhibiting such resilience, and is yet another example of an MST survivor who is working hard to pave her own path and not let others or her painful past do that for her. Telling her story here, and in much more detail in her own memoir, will surely help others not only to understand the complexities and viciousness of MST, but to continue or start their own healing journeys.

---

1 Lisa Carrington Firmin, "A call to action: Sexual assault and harassment in the military," *Military Times*, Dec. 2, 2020, https://www.militarytimes.com/opinion/commentary/2020/12/02/a-call-to-action-sexual-assault-and-harassment-in-the-military/.

CHAPTER 10

BROKEN TRUST

Victor Gonzalez

I didn't feel welcome in the Army and certainly did not feel safe in the combat environment, as I was always afraid of friendly fire. I had to worry about what the enemy was doing AND what could happen to me by my own brothers in arms.

Victor knew he was different and struggled with his sexual orientation for years before coming out as a gay man. Those of us in the Hispanic or Latino culture understand just how hard this can be, as mi gente doesn't typically rally around this type of declaration. One doesn't very easily tell the matriarch of the family, su madre, the strong mother who has raised three children on her own, something like this. This was probably harder for Victor to do than serving in combat in Afghanistan.

By the time he came out to his mother, at 17, Victor had already survived physical, sexual, and emotional abuse. While in the Army he would go on to endure unrelenting sexual harassment, a physical assault, betrayal by his fellow soldiers, a painful back injury, and more. After leaving the service, he would suffer a sexual assault while attending college and struggle with processing all the traumas he had experienced.

Nothing was easy for Victor, but even after cries for help through two suicide attempts almost a decade apart, he survives and excels, garnering three higher education degrees, starting his own business, and leading and helping others, especially his fellow vets. His story is a difficult one to tell, yet I must tell it so you can understand his trials and appreciate the significance of his triumphs.

Victor was born to Puerto Rican and Mexican American parents. Raised in Texas, he lived with his parents and two siblings in Corpus Christi until relocating to San Antonio abruptly when he was five, after a particularly bad altercation with his father, who threatened to kill them and locked them all in a back room. Abuse was common, and they were left frightened of what might come next. Victor's older brother managed to escape through a window and call the police, and his mother swept him and his siblings up and found the courage to leave the abusive man she was married to.

Living in fear, cringing at his father's physical and emotional abuse, Victor typically hid if he could when it occurred. "The first time I ever felt safe was in that police car that took us to the bus station so we could get away," he recalls. On the bus trip from Corpus to San Antonio, Victor remembers his mom telling him, "Mijo, you are okay, you are safe now."

The way the police officers handled the situation, and that first time feeling truly safe with them, made a lasting impression on the five-year-old. He had never before believed himself to be safe. Sadly, that sense of safety would be fleeting. When Victor was ten he was sexually assaulted by someone he knew. He never spoke about it until many years later as an adult, when he finally shared what had happened with his mother. Trusting others was getting harder and harder for him. The broken trust from the father who had harmed him instead of protecting him would resurface again and again in Victor's life, as others would break his trust and take advantage of his kind soul.

The family lived on San Antonio's south side and then moved to a more affluent part of town. They were not well off by any means, but his mom worked hard to support them and was able to get him into a good school, Alamo Heights. The new area and school were mostly white, with wealth, access, and success. He remembers being one of maybe five Latino kids, and that in the entire school there was only one African American kid. He stood out as a Latino, and soon he would stand out for another reason.

It was at Alamo Heights that he figured out that, as he told me, "You don't have to end life where you start it. I realized then that I don't have to be what my family has been. I can break that cycle of abuse." He became more involved in school and was part of the Junior ROTC program. That was also where he began to struggle with his sexual orientation. He wasn't sure if he was gay or not, and this ambiguity affected him for years.

Once he came to terms with being gay, he thought he was the only gay kid in school. This was in 1999-2000, and gay culture was not what it is today, especially in the Latino community. Victor says that the high school psychologist was great and helped him to understand and process his feelings. At 17 he came out, first to his friends. He was scared to tell his mother, but the school psychologist helped him prepare by providing him with an information packet that he could share with her on how to support a gay kid. She also introduced him to another student who was gay, and that really helped.

All this outstanding support from the school helped but Victor was still terrified of informing his mother. He wanted to tell her in person, but he lost his nerve. So one night he wrote her a long letter and hoped she would accept him. He left it, along with the information packet from the psychologist, for his mother to read in the morning while he was at school and work. He waited anxiously to hear what she thought, he so deeply wanted her acceptance.

He didn't hear anything, and at work in the afternoon a friend encouraged him to call his mother. When he did she said, "Victor, you are not telling me anything that I didn't already know. I love you no matter what." The relief he felt at that moment is beyond description. When he saw his mother later that day, she hugged him. His mom saved him the task of informing the rest of the family. Within a day the entire extended familia knew.

His siblings readily accepted him in both their words and their actions. But his mother's actions belied her initial words of acceptance, and their once strong and tight bond was fractured. They didn't have their special lunches together anymore; she didn't communicate with him as she had previously and, when she did, it was cruel and cut him to his core. She told him, for example, that she didn't want to see him holding hands with or kissing another man.

This initial coming out time was very hard on them both. Victor was just trying to find himself; he still didn't know who he really was. One New Year's Eve, he wasn't invited to a family gathering that they all always attended. "I was at a point in my life where I had gone through so much bullshit, never really experienced true happiness or joy, and getting my mother's acceptance was very important to me," he says. He really thought that his mother no longer loved him or accepted him because he was gay; he felt so alone.

During this very tumultuous time, at 17, Victor attempted suicide by swallowing an entire bottle of aspirin. He ended up throwing them all up, and afterwards he went straight to the one person who had supported him: the school psychologist. She helped both him and his mother to begin to understand what he was going through. It was clear that his mother did not truly grasp the depth of the issues he was dealing with.

Looking back, Victor says they both needed time apart, and that his mother needed time to absorb it all and possibly even to grieve the son she thought she had had, versus the son she had ended up with. He moved away. Three or four years would go by before their relationship would mend enough for them to begin to regain their intimacy. The interim fracture, the broken trust, healed over time, and they became as close as they had ever been.

After high school Victor held various jobs for several years, until he was informed that "we cannot advance you any further without a degree." In every case he showed he could lead and was placed in positions of increased responsibility, but without a degree he couldn't get the formal roles he was ready for. This is when he thought about joining the military. "It was either military service or debt," he says. His uncles served in both the Navy and the Army, and his brother joined the Air Force after college as an officer. So he prepared to enlist in the Army.

This was a huge decision, as it meant he would be going back into the closet as a gay man. He chose to do this, believing that it would be the easiest way for him to serve. "I wanted to serve so others wouldn't have to," he told me. He hoped he could fly under the radar. Not only did he sacrifice his identity to serve, but he lost his fiancé due to his decision. His fiancé couldn't tolerate Victor serving and told him their relationship was over.

He was 25 years old, and his fiancé was 38 at the time. Victor joined the military as a single man.

The services were under Don't Ask Don't Tell (DADT) at the time, in 2009. The policy prohibited military personnel from openly identifying as LGBTQ. The policy allowed him to serve, but he could not be out. After living an openly gay life since age 17, this was going to be hard for him.

And it was. The climate was not welcoming of gays, and harassment was commonplace. From the onset at boot camp he was harassed, teased, and bullied. His drill instructor asked him outright if he was gay, which was against the DADT policy. Victor served just over four years and, toward the end of his enlistment in 2011, the DADT policy was repealed. He led a secret life and didn't trust the repeal of the policy. "Just because the law was repealed didn't mean the culture changed," he pointed out. His opinion holds true for many gays who served and still are serving.

At boot camp he was constantly harassed, hazed, teased, and asked, "Are you gay?" When he told his drill instructor about the harassment, she asked him, "Well, are you?" On several occasions another male trainee would sing songs alleging that Victor wanted him, wanted to love him. The drill instructor made this young man sing the song in front of the entire unit with Victor standing right there. It was humiliating.

As luck would have it, Victor ran into this same trainee from basic while he was going through AIT (advanced individual training). Victor was walking and holding hands with his boyfriend off post, when he saw someone approaching. He told his boyfriend to stop holding hands and to remain neutral. As the person got closer, he was shocked to see that it was that same former trainee. Victor says that the man said he was sorry for how he had treated him at basic and admitted that he had had a thing for Victor and was acting out, as he was dealing with his own sexual orientation issues. Victor was livid and informed him that his behavior made it that much harder on gays in the military.

There are many parallels between Victor's harassment experiences and my own. As a Latina who joined the service in 1980, I too was met with harsh and persistent harassment. Much of the harassment in both cases tried to hide under the veil of "We were just kidding." The vicious jokes about gender and ethnicity were on par with what Victor encountered due to his sexual orientation. You would be totally degraded, and then everyone would laugh and say, "Just kidding." It was improper and totally unprofessional to hear remarks about our body parts, the size of his penis, the size of my breasts, and whether people like us should even serve.

The more Victor opened up and let me know how it really was, the more incensed I was that he would be subject to such degradation. He entered the service 20 years after I did and still was under the microscope, experiencing overt harassment and humiliation. How far have we really progressed? He says it quite clearly: "The military is not really that progressive regarding race, ethnicity, sexual orientation or gender. Senior military still do not accept women or gays." It has been a great façade to some extent that the military is a bastion of social progress and equal opportunity. One need only speak to any woman, any person of color, or any LGBTQ individual, or read any of multiple independent reviews, to learn the reality of the disparities that still exist. The one thing that is equal is the pay – but not the long journey up the ranks.

Victor never came out as gay in the military. He was forced out by a fellow soldier during his one-year deployment to Afghanistan. It was here that the hazing and harassment culminated in a physical assault. He was serving as a 92G, culinary specialist responsible for food service operations, providing hot meals at a COB (combat operations base) in southeastern Afghanistan.

Initially the harassment was not extreme, but on returning from leave he walked into a toxic environment. Since the sergeant in charge of food service was on leave for 30 days, Victor returned to lead the food operations during his absence. As he tells it, the entire atmosphere had changed drastically and everyone, especially the first sergeant, was constantly on him. Harassment was outright and overt. The first sergeant kept jumping on him, calling him a "fucking homo."

The hazing intensified, and one day an E-5 promotable tried to get in the back area of the food operations, where only food service personnel were authorized. Victor recalls that this soon-to-be-promoted to E-6 insisted on being allowed entry, just pushed past him, and assaulted him in the process, actually fracturing his hand. The altercation felt much longer than it was, as the sergeant continued to hurt Victor, twisting his arm and tossing out homophobic slurs. "I don't have to listen to you, you fucking faggot," was among the lesser things he yelled.

Apparently, while Victor was gone on leave, someone had gone through his things and found a flash drive that contained gay porn. Probably not the smartest thing for Victor to have brought on his deployment, but he says it was password protected and among his private possessions. The fact that this individual had purposely gone through his belongings was unbelievable to Victor. He says he felt like they were just looking for something to get him with, and his departure on leave was their opportunity.

Victor didn't trust the medic to explain how he had been injured. He told no one what really happened. He thought to himself, "Who would believe me? I'm just a private, and the dude who harassed and assaulted me was being promoted." Feeling totally isolated, Victor asked his boss (E-7) to relocate him from the COB. He got support from his leadership, who agreed to get him out of that environment and told him to shut down the food service operations and "let them eat MREs." But that support and belief in Victor wouldn't last.

A few days later, Victor's E-7 confronted the E-6 who had harassed and assaulted him. "He was all up in his face, and I just stood there, hiding behind my E-7," recalls Victor. "I remember he asked me, 'Why are you hiding?'" It was at that moment that Victor regressed to being a child undergoing physical and sexual abuse. Compounding the situation was when an investigation was conducted and his leadership later backed off their support. It was hard for Victor to understand as everyone denied all the harassment and hazing as well as the physical assault. It became the private's word against the sergeants and everyone else. The private lost. The sergeant would go on not only to be promoted but to receive an Army Commendation Medal.

It was at a very low time in Victor's life. No one believed him, and his own boss had pulled the rug out from under him. He felt a deep betrayal, even more so when he found out that his leadership had known beforehand about the flash drive, but never warned Victor about the situation he could be walking into. No one had his back, and no one was going to protect him. He would have to do that all by himself.

It was at this time that he attempted suicide, for a second time, at the main FOB. He tried to use his own gun on himself, going so far as to have the barrel in his mouth, but then stopped himself. What prevented him from taking his life was his mother; he could never do that to her. He was put on suicide watch and remained at the main FOB for a couple of months, until he was cleared by the psychologist. He then was reassigned not back home but to another FOB.

At the new FOB he went outside the wire twice and both times was afraid of friendly fire. He would ask a friend to watch his back. "I didn't feel welcome in the Army and certainly did not feel safe in the combat environment, as I was always afraid of friendly fire," he told me. "I had to worry about what the enemy was doing *and* what could happen to me by my own brothers in arms."

At this second FOB, he worked serving meals to about 400 people daily. He also trained with local Afghans. There were about 150 Afghan soldiers there, and twelve workers that he interacted with daily. He soon learned about a practice called *bacha bazi* in Afghanistan, that involved the use of boys for entertainment and sex by men. Victor was horrified. He recalls asking his translator to explain the practice to him and was told, "The boys are used for sex, for fun, and the women are used for reproduction." He began to question how the United States could be helping people who practiced this. He remembered how devasting his own sexual abuse at a young age had been, and the psychological wounds he still bore. Victor was deeply affected and simply couldn't wrap his head around this practice.

Something happened in Afghanistan that Victor learned about much later, after he returned stateside. It left him profoundly conflicted. It was the sexual assault by an E-6 against three younger soldiers, two E-1s and an E-2. According to Victor, the E-6 perpetrator raped the three younger soldiers, was convicted, and was sent to Leavenworth. But Victor remembers the soldiers back in Afghanistan, seeing them come through the chow line, seeing the look of defeat on their faces. He is pained as he recalls this as he had been raped before and knew the feelings of shame, defeat, and isolation. "I should have said something," he said to me. "I understood that look. I have had that look." Knowing he couldn't have prevented their rape gives him little comfort. He feels deeply that he could have spoken with them, helped them deal with what had happened. To this day he struggles with what he didn't do to try to help those three soldiers after their sexual assault.

Towards the end of his time in Afghanistan, Victor barely responded to attacks. He just kept working and, when forced to seek shelter, he didn't run but walked, as if there were not an attack ongoing. While deployed, Victor sustained an injury to his back, which would later require fusion of several discs in his spine. His attitude was not good, and he was in pain, tired, dejected from all the harassment and distrust. "I just didn't give a shit," he says. He was physically and mentally checked out. His year was about up. He returned to the States, where he would ultimately undergo surgery.

Once on post stateside, he would once again be met with harassment. He was called names such as queen, duchess, fucking diva; the climate was toxic for him. And he was still in great pain from his back injury. He was in both physical and emotional pain, struggling just to get through the days. A kind E-7 at home base provided Victor with all the new regulations about DADT and told him: "I just want you to be aware of your rights as a man in the military." If only more were as tolerant. Another, less tolerant E-7 told him to "get the fuck out of his DFAC." This was Victor's life, being caught in the middle between those who were professional and accepted him and those who never would. It was an exhausting position to be in, on the receiving end of relentless harassment and vicious name-calling, day in and day out.

It was about this time, in 2013, that Victor finally had surgery to fuse the vertebrae in his lower spine, after countless doctor's appointments with no one really listening to him about the severity of the pain he was in. When he finally met the doctor who would do the surgery in Bethesda, Maryland, she informed him that she couldn't believe he was still walking around with the damage to his lower spine.

When he returned after having surgery, he was faced with an allegation that he had sexually assaulted a fellow soldier. The allegation was that Victor had grabbed another man's buttocks in the restroom. The accuser was someone Victor had recently chewed out for not doing his job properly. They were the same rank, but Victor was senior in position. Victor says it was a made-up accusation, further evidence that the leadership and his fellow soldiers were retaliating against him for being gay and a stickler for regulations. According to Victor, his own sergeant told him that the trumped-up charges were payback from leadership for his having stood up to the sergeant major and many others, quoting the regulations to them about work and policies surrounding DADT.

Victor recalls that, after he informed his senior enlisted that, according to regulations, he didn't have to discuss his sex life, he was told that he didn't have the right to *not* talk about his sexual orientation or the right to force his orientation on others. Victor was shocked at what this senior enlisted man was telling him, as it violated existing policy. At the end of the day, it didn't matter that Victor knew the regs and quoted them accurately. He still received nonjudicial punishment in the form of an Article 15. His own officer leadership said they believed Victor, but that they had to take the action they did. He passed out a suspended sentence resulting in fourteen days of extra duty. Once again Victor was not believed, and the little trust he had in his leadership evaporated.

After this, Victor was done serving his country. The harassment never stopped, and he just couldn't stay. He recalled that some leadership was following policy and holding people accountable in the fair treatment of gays, but many others were not. His physical injury and his emotional wounds were too deep to remain. He ended up with a 100 percent VA disability.

Victor went back to school, earning a bachelor's degree in business administration in management from The University of Texas at San Antonio. It is here where our paths crossed. I had just stood up the new department of

Veteran and Military Affairs (VMA) at UTSA and had been doing more and more engagement with and on behalf of student veterans. Victor was the president of the Student Veterans Association and advocated fiercely for student vets. So fiercely that he was chastised by some for the manner in which he spoke with senior university leaders.

I stepped in and offered to mentor him and provide professional development. He had what I thought was a huge chip on his shoulder and resentment of leadership, but I also saw huge potential. He turned me down and said he didn't need professional development. Frankly, he was offended by my offer; he was really angry. A couple of months went by, and he stopped in and asked me, "Is your offer to help me still open?" I said yes, and that began a professional relationship that exists to this day.

Of course, I had no way of knowing Victor's story. Now that I do, his behavior in college makes sense. He experienced so much while serving. It was amazing to me that he could even function, much less be successful. It wasn't easy, as his experiences with leadership had not been good, but I provided the professional support and tough love he needed. I never broke my promise to help him develop professionally and have always been there for him. After the broken trust he experienced in the Army, it was something that he appreciated and respected.

I never knew that Victor had been drugged and sexually assaulted while attending college. I didn't learn this until we sat down to have the interviews for this book. I was stunned. It happened at an off-campus party. He did go to the emergency room to receive treatment, but he refused to report it. The guilt and shame from his childhood all came back. Victor has truly been victimized throughout his life, but he is no victim. He relates his story now, with all its pain, in order that others can learn they are not alone and that there is life after trauma.

So how does he cope with all that he has been through? He gives credit to a particular person who asked him, "How long are you going to take to get some help? Your mask is breaking down." Shocking as that was, it was the catalyst for him to begin therapy and finally to address his past trauma. He has tried various types of therapy over the years. Initially his experience with the VA health services was not good, and he sought therapy with a nonprofit specially tailored to assist veterans. It was here that he started EMDR therapy and met a good therapist. He is working on his coping skills, on how to address and process his feelings and experiences. He uses various techniques such as tapping, meditation, and breathing.

"I am now with community health through the VA," he reports, "seeing a private therapist, not one employed by the VA. And my therapist is gay and we have some in-depth conversations." He says he must give it to the VA as they are really trying to enhance support for LGBTQ veterans. His VA doctor is gay, and Victor can openly speak with him about his health as he feels comfortable doing so.

Victor has been quite successful, an amazing feat once you learn his story. He started his own company, V.E.J. Gonzalez Consulting even before he graduated from college. He organized and led the student vet association to much success. He testified before the Texas legislature about supporting veterans and their families in higher education. And much more. After college, he worked for a while in a leadership role as part of an executive team as a life insurance division manager and assistant general agent. He has since left that organization to focus on growing his own consulting business. "As veterans, our service to America is never done!" declares Victor. "We must always pay it forward and give back to those who come after us." He wants to help others, especially veterans. He believes that more authentic trainings for active-duty personnel, veterans' groups, and others would go a long way to help them understand about MST, go toward helping people understand how to protect their soldiers, and how to respond in healthier and healing ways.

Telling his story took tremendous courage on Victor's part and is a running start to helping educate and inform others. He has the support of his family, his bond with his mother is as strong as it ever was, and his siblings have always been there for him. Victor deserves our respect for sharing his traumatic experiences. He is not alone in what he went through, and neither are you.

CHAPTER 11

SHOCK AND AWE

JC Jackson

What's interesting is that I would say 99 percent of the men that I have had issues with when it comes to sexual assault and harassment have all been men in their forties and fifties. And almost all were white males.

JC Jackson traveled all over the world during her seven years of service in the Air Force. In fact, she served three tours of duty overseas. For her, this was one of the positive things about being in military. She loved the traveling, learning about different cultures, and the friends she made. If it hadn't been for having to fend off older white males at three different bases, the positives might have outweighed the negatives. She might even have stayed in longer.

I feel personally responsible for the abuse that JC underwent. I know I wasn't really personally responsible, but she was one of mine. She was one of my ROTC cadets at The University of Texas at San Antonio (UTSA) when I was a ROTC Commander. The commander-cadet relationship can go fairly deep, and it meant something to both JC and me, still does.

She came to our detachment at UTSA as a transfer student from community college. I tried to prepare her and her fellow cadets for what they might encounter as young officers, junior leaders in the military. I shared with them lessons that I had learned in my long military career. I even spoke to JC about the harassment she might endure as a young woman in what is still a man's military. Little did I know that she would experience not only harassment, but sexual assault as well.

JC was raised in California and relocated to Texas at nineteen, along with her family. She was the youngest of three siblings. She began attending community college and working. She had a friend in high school in California who was in the Civil Air Patrol and working toward a dream of attending the Air Force Academy. Her friend informed her that if she didn't get into the Academy, she would go ROTC. JC says the military had always interested her, but she had no real experience with it. Her father served in the Navy, but that was when JC was very young, and she therefore had no real experience with being a military dependent.

She didn't even know the difference between enlisted and officers and was very naïve about military service. While attending community college at St Phillip's in San Antonio, she worked as a Tae Kwon Do instructor and was a third-degree black belt. She expressed interest in the military to a fellow instructor, an active-duty Air Force major. He encouraged JC to pursue ROTC at a four-year institution and even accompanied her to an Air Force ROTC open house at UTSA since her father was still back in California.

It was at that open house that she committed to joining the program. All she knew was that she would have a job upon graduation. When she informed her father of her decision, he congratulated her on going Air Force, as he said that was the best branch for women. He had no way of knowing what his daughter would be subjected to as a young officer in the Air Force.

She spent two and a half years in ROTC, graduated from UTSA, and was commissioned as a second lieutenant in December 2010. But she had to wait until June 2011 before going active, due to the long lead time for an open slot at technical training for her career field. She was very fortunate to get her first choice of career fields, Intelligence.

It was on to Korea for the first of three overseas assignments she would have before separating as a captain. She was made a flight commander upon arriving and an ISR (Intelligence, Surveillance and Reconnaissance) operations commander. At Osan, Korea, she oversaw 62 personnel. "I wasn't a fan of the environment in Korea," she told me. "I liked my friends but not my work climate. It was negative, almost as if the squadron had a black cloud over it. I had an immediate sense of dread when I walked into the place; I picked up on the negative energy." She soon found out why. It appeared that a few of the senior leaders did not get along. When that happens, it all sort of just rolls downhill. JC recalls that the personnel in the squadron got dumped on a lot.

Although she did not personally have any bad experiences regarding MST there, she remembers that several of her female friends did. She did encounter gendered comments while in Korea. She recalls one incident near the time she was PCSing (permanent change of station) out of there. One of the sergeants made a comment about her to others. "She's one of the good lieutenants," he said. "She doesn't sleep around." It was stated like a compliment to her. JC spoke up and informed the group that she knew the other female lieutenants, and they didn't sleep around either. And she went on: "So how come you don't talk about the male officers this way? I know for a fact that some of them sleep around." It was 2013, and her point was that it is not okay to speak about women in this manner, and to attempt to get the men to see that.

Another incident occurred in Korea around the same time. She was near departure from her yearlong tour, on base, headed to join a tour. It was very early in the morning, still dark as the bus was due to leave for the off-base tour before sunrise. She was walking to board the bus, it was in her sights, when she noticed a very drunk Korean military member walking toward her. He stared at her, made eye contact, and then made a beeline for her. "He was charging at me like a bull," JC told me. "I spread out my arms and legs and shouted as loud as I could: 'No, no, no.' The word stopped him in his tracks like he had hit a wall."

She departed Korea and headed to Aviano, Italy for her second overseas assignment. There she led a five-member analysis team that supported fighter aircraft operations. JC found that leading a small team was much different, and in some ways much harder, than what she had led in Korea. Small group dynamics was just the beginning of the issues she would encounter in Italy. It was at Aviano that she encountered her first truly negative experience in the Air Force. She found herself in an extremely toxic workplace environment, so much so that she contemplated suicide. And this was before she experienced two MST incidents.

There was a superior officer that was as toxic as they come. JC describes him as a narcissistic a-hole who resented her small team. The entire unit worked in a secret facility, but JC's team worked inside of that within an even more secure, top secret SCIF (sensitive compartmented information facility). She led the team in conducting research and analysis. Basically, her team carried out intelligence analysis for the fighter aircraft missions.

Analysis wasn't her strong suit yet, but instead of giving her mentorship this superior officer threatened them all, all the time. "I honestly think he got some kind of sick pleasure from humiliating people in front of everyone, and from personally tearing them down," she says. According to JC, he would throw out daggers about them being the worst analysts he'd ever seen, but he never provided any guidance on how to improve.

JC recalls that a senior enlisted was just as bad. Instead of good cop, bad cop, it was bad cop, bad cop. And JC and her team took the brunt of the terrible treatment and harassment. When she further investigated the situation, she found that it didn't matter who worked in the TS SCIF; it seemed they were always treated with resentment. She didn't think the harassment was due to her being a woman; she remembers the superior officer treating everyone with disrespect.

Compounding the issue was that the superior officer was great at the technical aspects of his job, and the pilots loved him. Additionally, JC remembers that another officer more senior to her was a complete pushover, couldn't lead or stand up for anything or anyone. She had no real support in her chain of command.

The superior officer told her multiple times that she was a terrible leader and threatened to fire her on numerous occasions. JC walked on eggshells, and the environment became more and more toxic and untenable. She dreaded going to work. She was on her own to try to protect herself and her team. She regrets that she was so caught up in her own despair that she didn't provide the top cover her team needed. It became just too much, day in and day out.

The situation was so bad that JC even tried to get out of the Air Force early. But she couldn't get out because so many intel officers had already taken the early out programs. For the first time in her life, she started to craft a plan to commit suicide. She felt completely alone and mentally exhausted. She was trapped in this position for one and a half more years. It was maddening. She admits that she has had suicidal thoughts since the age of 13, but this was the first time she ever made a plan.

The morning she planned to go through with it, a dear friend who was also in the military called her, recognized something was off, and immediately invited her to come over. The friend was there for her at a very low moment in her life. She so desperately needed someone. Her friend became a lifeline. JC never told her friend that she had contemplated suicide and remains grateful to her for her kindness and support. Further, she states that suicide is never the answer and acknowledges that both therapy and a solid support network are important.

After that unknowing intervention by a friend and getting advice on leadership from her father and another individual, she was better armed to make changes in her life and in her leadership style. She no longer allowed toxic leaders to affect her the way she used to. She listened, kept what she needed, and dumped the rest. It saved her sanity and enhanced her ability to lead others and ultimately to provide top cover to those junior to her.

While at Aviano, JC experienced sexual harassment and sexual assault. The incidents occurred with both enlisted and officer personnel and demonstrated to her how some men acted entitled regarding sexual harassment, with sexualized banter, unwelcome advances, and sex with much younger women.

Several friends from her own squadron and another all went out drinking and partying in the city center. JC recalls that she didn't dress up; her hair was up in a messy bun and she was wearing clothing that completely covered her. Right away she noticed a senior enlisted member homed in on her, making comments and snide remarks. He was not from her squadron.

The group ended up at a popular bar. There was another senior enlisted man from the base there who was celebrating, most likely a retirement, and his elderly father was there with him. JC and her friends were sitting at a table with long benches similar to a picnic table. Another sergeant from her home base was trying to speak to her, so she straddled the bench to look at him. The senior enlisted who had zeroed in on her backed himself into her crotch and said, "Oh, I like that." Everyone saw it and heard it and not one person said a word, not any enlisted or officer there.

The comments became even more sexualized. "I was so shocked and disgusted that I got up to leave," recalls JC. "I felt so completely invalidated, that I wasn't supported." Her team in Korea had always had her back, and her friends there would have stood up for her. For JC this was a betrayal; no one stood up for her here. No one said anything about the inappropriate conduct that they all had witnessed. This was the first time that JC realized she had to watch her own back, she had no back up.

As she was leaving the bar and walking away from the table, the senior enlisted man's father, who was in attendance for the retirement celebration, slapped her on the buttocks. "I turned around, completely shocked," says JC. The senior who had been sexually harassing her throughout the evening said, "Well, you do have a nice ass." The senior enlisted's father, who was in his seventies, remarked, "And I can get away with it because I'm old."

Again, no one said anything. JC herself wishes now that she had spoken up or done something right at that moment. But she was so shocked by everything that had happened that she just left. She called a friend the next day, and JC says his first question was, "Well, what were you wearing?" She told him and he said, "Well, I've seen you in those jeans, JC. I mean, what did you expect was going to happen? Men are men."

JC was horrified at the complete lack of support from her supposed friend. She felt like what she wore should never be the issue, and that the men in question were much older and had a sense of entitlement. "I didn't report the senior because he had a prominent position on base, and he was like a bro," she told me. "I also knew if I reported him, it would likely not end well for me." She was also aware that she would be ostracized; with sadness, she remembered how no one had had her back.

Her second incident involving MST occurred soon after she had pinned on captain. JC says it involved a senior field grade officer who was two ranks higher than she was. He was in the guard and part of a group visiting the base in Italy. One evening the group's intel officer invited JC and her friends out for drinks. She remembers that while they were drinking, she made some sexual jokes. She was drinking and trying to fit in with the guys. She caught herself and realized what she was doing, stopped with the jokes, and was careful about how much she drank.

However, it appeared that she had already made an impression on the lieutenant colonel. He started to try to get her to drink more, putting more drinks in front of her even when she said she didn't want any more. He began to make odd comments. She took any drinks he provided and dumped them out when he wasn't looking. She became more and more uncomfortable with his actions, so much so that she pulled a friend aside and told him that the senior field grade officer was either trying to get her drunk or might be drugging her drinks.

Since JC hadn't really drunk all that much, she told her friend, "If I start acting drunk, lock me up in my car and call the first sergeant." Her friend told her that he had noticed the field grade officer's attentions and had been keeping an eye on him. He was just as worried. Nothing transpired that night.

Over the next couple of weeks, the field grade officer began to send her creepy messages, comments like "Let's be besties on FB." The emails persisted and were full of inappropriate sexual innuendo, especially coming from a field grade officer to a company grade officer.

When JC did mention his behavior to members of his team, they told her, "he's known as a creeper, but you aren't going to say anything, are you?" She asked for advice from the base's sexual assault response coordinator and was told that she needed to specifically state that she wanted him to stop sending her messages, and to keep good notes about each occurrence. JC did exactly that. The field grade officer said he thought she wanted him, but he stopped sending her messages and left her alone. She didn't report it, since his behavior stopped when she asked him to stop messaging her.

Just before she was due to PCS from Aviano, she found out that the senior enlisted who had made very explicit sexualized comments to her had done it before. She heard both enlisted personnel and officers sharing stories about him. They all had stories involving the senior. She left Aviano in the wake of a toxic workplace, a near suicide attempt, and two incidents of military sexual trauma. She had enough of overseas. She was headed stateside, to San Angelo, Texas.

In several ways, Texas was like a breath of fresh air for JC. She was closer to home and family. She was also very happy; her workplace environment was much healthier than she had previously experienced. And she loved her actual job; she loved teaching. Finally, she was involved in a wonderful Bible study and was a volunteer to help at-risk teens. Her life was looking up, her professional and personal missions were of value, and she was making a difference.

A short-notice combat tour to Afghanistan interrupted that tranquil existence, requiring pre-deployment training, prerequisites, gathering of supplies, and combat gear. She had to execute all the standard relocation actions associated with a six-month tour on an extremely fast timeline. The short notice was due to someone else falling out due to medical reasons. JC was tapped to go in their place. She was ready; this was what she had trained for.

While undergoing training to prepare for deployment, JC would experience the only incident of sexual assault that she officially reported. She came to learn how stressful reporting could be. It was quite a lengthy process that took a little over a year to complete. And it was complex, complete with difficulties surrounding having adequate legal representation from the onset. Stuck in Afghanistan during the first part of the inquiry, she also experienced sexual harassment while waiting for her investigation.

The sexual assault occurred on the last night of a two-week-long training prior to deploying. Several individuals went out to dinner and then planned to go for drinks to mark the end of training. JC noticed a man sitting by himself, not engaging with anyone. She knew he was a senior enlisted member in the Air National Guard but did not know him. She asked him if he wanted to join her group.

JC says that immediately she noticed something was off about him. She had a bad, icky feeling about him. He was a bit too handsy, so she changed seats to put further distance between them. He followed and sat across from her, kept bumping her feet, and said, "Oh, we're playing footsie." She didn't know how to react, so she just kept her feet away from him and laughed nervously.

When he got up to get a drink, JC got up and moved. She then explained to the group that she didn't want him anywhere near her. They agreed to try to keep him from her. The group moved to the bar area, and this is when JC recalls that the sergeant came up behind her and began to rub her shoulders and lower back. She told him, "You're in my space. You need to back off." And he did. For a while.

The group went on to a few other bars. At one, two male captains told JC to sit between them, to put more distance between her and the sergeant. Everyone had noticed that he seemed to zero in on her, by the way he leered and tried to touch her. His behavior was quite brazen. When she went to the bathroom, he told one of the captains that he was trying to get her to sleep with him. Once she heard that from one of her friends, JC says she was shocked, as he was an enlisted member, and that would be fraternization at a minimum and something more if he actually tried to have sex with her. She goes on to say, "I was fairly drunk at this point, so that would have been considered rape had he been successful."

Somehow, he got close enough to grope her buttocks. JC remembers pushing his hands away. Towards the end of the evening, just prior to departing the bar, he stood waiting for her outside the women's restroom. JC wouldn't come out. The bartender came in and noticed JC hovering in the restroom. Hearing JC's predicament, she called over a bouncer and they both escorted her to a waiting taxi.

"What's interesting is that I would say ninety-nine percent of the men that I have had issues with when it comes to sexual assault and harassment have all been men in their forties and fifties," she observes. "And almost all were white males." She said they all acted as if they were entitled to her, to say and do whatever they wanted. This master sergeant was similar to others who harassed her.

She informed her roommate, also a sergeant, about what had happened, and she encouraged JC to report him, as he was headed to Afghanistan to be a first sergeant. How many young enlisted women would he be around, with him in a position of authority in a deployed location? JC knew she had to say something. Her roommate told her to write down everything that occurred. JC did that and contacted those who had been there, to see if they would be willing to be interviewed if she reported it. They all agreed.

JC contacted her flight and squadron commanders back at home base. She was surprised at how supportive they were. She went to another base to be interviewed and was again surprised at how kind everyone was. "I expected to be questioned and semi-blamed for my own actions," she says. But she was informed that it wasn't her fault. What did baffle JC was that since the incident occurred at a training base and not hers or the sergeant's, she would be assigned a JAG from his base but would be assigned a victim advocate from her own base. That she would get a JAG from his base seemed odd to her.

The case dragged on throughout her deployment, and for seven months afterwards. However, the sergeant's deployment as a first sergeant was immediately stopped. According to JC, her assigned JAG made it quite clear that he didn't believe her and would rather have been representing the sergeant. In fact, she found out that the sergeant had told the OSI that he thought she was into him. Recall that he was enlisted and JC was a company grade officer.

Once JC informed her victim's advocate that she was planning on contacting a member of Congress due to the lack of support from her attorney, he was removed from her case and a more senior officer took over. This officer who stepped in informed JC that she had a very good case, with lots of witnesses' statements. "Not only did every witness back up my story about his predatory behavior, but I discovered he had been accused of harassment twice before," JC recalls.

Finally, more than a year after she had reported the incident, it was determined that the sergeant had been out of line, and JC was informed that he would receive nonjudicial punishment, more than likely an Article 15. She never knew what actually took place, other than that his deployment had been cancelled. She felt she might at least have prevented him from harassing others in a deployed setting.

It was difficult for JC to deal with the stress of the case while deployed. That came with its own challenges, such as further sexual harassment and pursuit by men, to include a married man. At some point, she even wore a fake engagement ring to see if that deterred men from asking her out and making unwanted advances. It didn't work and, in fact, it backfired, since some men saw pursuing her as a challenge.

One officer, a married field grade officer with kids, kept sending her messages. Finally, she responded one day with, "Your wife probably wouldn't like you sending a single female and junior officer inappropriate messages." JC says he responded with "Oh, you misinterpreted." Another, a contractor, frequently touched her on the legs and waist in the workplace. He asked her out in front of everyone, probably thinking she couldn't decline in front of everyone, but she did. There were others who just made the workplace environment toxic with their behavior, yelling, cussing people out, talking about shooting themselves or others. She tried not to let it all get to her, but it was emotionally draining.

It was time to exit the military. After working as a government contractor for various organizations since departing the Air Force, JC is now working for a company that is not affiliated with the government and is truly enjoying her training role, where she instructs others.

JC says that her experiences both in and out of the military have left her distrusting of men, especially white males over forty. She understands that this distrust stems somewhat from her experiences while serving her country and continues to pursue therapy with a nonprofit specifically tailored to assist veterans with PTSD and MST. Speaking out more about her experiences has helped her.

One huge accomplishment has been publishing her own book, *The Myth of Adulting: Everyone's Just Winging It.* She describes the book as sort of a guide for how to be an adult and says it discusses identity crises, career changes, depression, anxiety, spirituality, singleness, suicide, and MST, among other topics. The book is written from material in fifteen years of personal journals. It is a quick but insightful read that can help others understand that they are not alone in facing some of life's toughest challenges.

JC's courage to publish deeply personal information about herself, and to share her MST experiences in this book, are but two examples of her wanting to help others. Life is tough. JC found a way to get past it all and offers us, through piercing honesty and a touch of humor, advice and tips on how to be kind to ourselves as we navigate our own life journeys.

CHAPTER 12

TRIPLE THREAT

Sanchez[1]

As a Latina and a woman, I always felt like I had to work extra hard just to be recognized or be known. I am constantly on guard and in competition mode. All I ever want is to be recognized for my work and the value I bring.

In the fall of 2021, the Air Force Inspector General released the Independent Disparity Review (DR). It was an eye-opening report exploring disparities in the service among gender and ethnic groups. It revealed that

From CY15 to CY20, [Latinos] had 21% lower odds of holding enlisted leadership positions, were 34% less likely to have been a squadron/group commander, and 42% less likely to have been promoted in the O4-O6 [grades] than their White peers...On average between 2015 and 2020, females were underrepresented as squadron/group and wing commanders across components.[2]

These disparities and others listed in the DR are significant and can affect one's rise up the ranks, specifically for Latino officers who are trying to

---

1 Sanchez is a pseudonym for this active-duty airman.

2 See "The Inspector General Department of the Air Force Report of Inquiry (S8918P) Disparity Review," September 2021, pp. 5-6, https://apps.dtic.mil/sti/citations/ADA424597.

advance to the ranks of major through colonel. The DR cited survey data from active-duty airmen and guardians and summarized that "Hispanic/Latino members reported a sense their accomplishments are overlooked and described situations where they were subjected to disparaging slurs." Additionally, surveys revealed that the "good old boy or bro network exists in the Air Force, particularly in male dominated units, and is a barrier to females."

The fact that Sanchez even made major and is a field grade officer is a huge achievement and cannot be overstated. Not only is she a woman, and a Latina, but she is also gay and there are many that serve who view her as a triple threat. To whom? To the predominantly white male heterosexual majority who are in the highest levels of leadership within the Air Force. She is truly different than they are. She is a great example of true diversity within the ranks.

The Air Force says it values diversity, but the DR issued in 2021 clearly shows that they have a long way to go in many areas, including recruitment, retention, professional development, and selections for key billets like command or professional military education. In fact, what I find appalling is that I identified much of what was recently revealed regarding Latinos in the Air Force's disparity review almost twenty years ago in an Air War College research paper titled "Hispanics: An Untapped Leadership Resource." Not much has changed, I am sad to say.[3]

Sanchez stands out. She cannot hide that she is a woman or a Latina. But she still conceals from many that she is gay, despite the repeal in 2011 of Don't Ask Don't Tell. The culture changes have not caught up with the changes in law.

Not being able to bring your whole, authentic self to work each and every day is exhausting. That is the workplace environment that Sanchez is currently in as an active-duty airman. She loves the Air Force, had always wanted to serve to continue her family's legacy. Her father served in the Air Force, and she was exposed to the military at a very young age, living

---

3 See Lisa C. Firmin, Col., USAF, *"Hispanics: An Untapped Leadership Resource,"* Air War College, 2002 https://apps.dtic.mil/sti/citations/ADA424597.

in enlisted housing at many bases. She clearly understood the distinction between officer and enlisted. Most of her friends were enlisted kids. In addition to her father, her grandfather and great-great grandfather also served. She comes from a long line of military, but she was the first woman to serve and the first person in the family to get a commission and become an officer.

Sanchez was born in Illinois but grew up all over the world, in Panama, Spain, London, and the Netherlands. Her family was a global one, and life was exciting and always evolving. Her father was raised in the suburbs of Chicago; her mother was born in Spain but raised in Peru. Sanchez had two older brothers born in other countries. When she was 15, the family met with a devastating loss as one of her brothers passed away at 23 due to an allergic reaction to medication. This affected Sanchez at a deep level.

During her high school years her father was stationed at an airbase in Europe. There was no high school on that base; the nearest school was two hours away. So she and her family made the decision for her to attend a boarding school in England. Her fellow students were diplomatic and Department of Defense kids. The school was paid for by DoD, including tuition, travel, lodging, and food. She says it was as if she went to college at fourteen. Adulting before her time.

After a couple of years the family was relocated to the Netherlands, and it was there that she graduated from high school and garnered a highly coveted four-year scholarship to go to any school in the United States that offered Air Force ROTC. She selected a university in Texas due to her niece being in the same city. This was the daughter of her deceased brother, and Sanchez wanted to be close to family, especially her niece.

She excelled in her ROTC program, assuming various leadership roles, culminating as vice commander of the cadet wing. However, she got into a bit of trouble immediately upon arrival at summer field training. She was navigating her way to the barracks and saw that someone had dropped a wallet containing personal IDs. She thought she should turn it in to someone. So she deviated from going to her barracks, found someone in a leadership role ready to hand in the wallet and, as she says, "I got my butt handed to me." She was told that she didn't have permission to speak and that she was supposed to have gone directly to her barracks.

Also at field training, she noticed that she was the only one making the beds in her women's barracks area. Everyone should have been helping. She was the only Latina; all the other women were white. Sanchez didn't say anything; she was trying to be a team player. So she just made the beds. She didn't want to create any conflict. She kept her mouth shut and tried hard to fit in. She has at times been accused of being the stereotypical passionate Latina. She got teased a bit more than the others. Sanchez says that it is just who she is: When she feels strongly about something, she speaks up and routinely gets accused of showing too much emotion. She learned early to be on guard and to watch how she phrases things to others.

While attending ROTC and throughout college and her first six years in the military, she didn't know she was gay. In fact, she didn't come out until she had served six years active duty. It didn't hit her like a ton of bricks, but was more like a gradual, comfortable realization of finally knowing who she really was.

In college she struggled a bit with her sexuality and with just letting loose and having fun. She had lived most of her life overseas, and returning to the States to attend college was quite a shock. Living overseas certainly broadens your lived experiences, but you sometimes feel as if you are a bit behind what is happening in the States.

"I felt I wanted to fit in," she says. "All my peers were having the time of their lives. Two of my fellow cadets came on to me." She went out with a couple, messed around a little, tried to get off the sidelines and into the game a bit, catch up like the others. One of the cadets wanted to have sex with her, to go all the way. She bluntly asked him if he was ready to be a dad. He clearly wasn't, as he backed off and didn't pressure her again.

She went on to do well in college and graduated with a bachelor's degree in psychology. Then it was off to Air and Space Basic Course (ASBC) to learn more about being a warrior in the Air Force. It was at ASBC that she first experienced sexual harassment. She had been in the service less than a month. She was barely 22 years old.

There is the formal part of the ASBC program and then there is the informal part, extracurricular activities including what many call "mandatory fun." One is expected to participate, to be part of the group. It was at one of these "mandatory fun" events, basically hanging out in a rowdy bar in the basement of the Officers' Club, where Sanchez was welcomed into the officer ranks.

Alcohol flowed freely, and debauchery was the norm. Drinking was certainly considered part of the informal experience. Sanchez was at the club, as she knew it was all part of the overall informal game. While there, she saw another woman officer pass out from drinking too much. That wasn't going to happen to Sanchez, as she stuck with nonalcoholic drinks.

The music was good and the company seemed okay too, if you ignored the heavy drinking, the raunchy banter, and the fact that men outnumbered women. Sanchez tried to relax and fit in, and she danced with some of her classmates. Another officer, a field grade officer three ranks above her, a major, zeroed in on her. Sanchez was a second lieutenant, the lowest rank in the officer corps, and literally brand new to active duty.

This major, a combative trainer and not a small person, wanted to dance with her and pulled her in very close. "He gripped me so hard, he left little marks. He told me to dance on him." Sanchez says she just froze. She was so surprised and a little bit scared that this major groped her like that, and she wondered if this was how it was going to be in the military. He was so brash and totally at ease with what he did.

She recovered soon enough and told him to leave her alone. She also told him that her dad was a cop. "I didn't think about reporting him at all," she recalls. "Being open about doing that was not encouraged. Besides, who would I have told? We didn't have a SARC [Sexual Assault Response Coordinator]. I didn't feel educated enough about reporting it."

Following ASBC, she went on to technical training for her career field. This was Personnel, her first choice. At tech training she found one other Latina, so she wasn't so alone as she had been at ROTC field training. At her first duty assignment in the United States, Sanchez experienced more microaggressions and hassles for being different.

She made a road trip from the base to another city several hours away to drop off an airman who was deploying. On the way back her car broke down, so she called a friend to pick her up. At work the next day, she used her lunch hour to call down to where her car was, to see about getting it fixed and returned to her. According to Sanchez, she was told she was too focused on personal problems at work. It didn't matter that the only reason she had made the trip was to drop off a fellow airman for deployment. Sanchez says she didn't get the care and feeding that most people get in the military from their chain of command. She always seems to be the odd person out.

One time, when another troop was sick and home alone, he got meals delivered to him for the duration of his illness. When Sanchez was sick, no one checked on her or brought her anything. This went against all that she had been taught about taking care of your own. Most units do take care of troops in some way when they are sick or down and out for whatever reason. That is what Sanchez had liked so much about the military: that it was a family and everyone was supposed to help each other. Unfortunately, that hasn't been the case for her.

It is a lesson she had to learn the hard way, and it resolves her always to put her people first and never let them fend for themselves. She still finds herself isolated from her leadership and continues to act on her own. She also says people tend to flip things around due to their own prejudices and beliefs. For example, she recalls that one of her commanders would invite airmen to his church, but never her. She always felt she was being excluded for being gay.

She is very selective about who she discusses her sexual orientation with and says that anything and everything can be used against you. This is what she meant by people flipping things around. Sanchez says most people just assume she is heterosexual and talk openly about her being with a man. She just lets them talk and corrects people only if she feels she is in a safe environment and that whoever is there can be trusted. She finds it interesting that her sex life continues to be a topic of discussion in the workplace and believes it has no place there.

Her annual evaluations and recommendations for selective assignments have been impacted by her being perceived as a triple threat. Unsure if it is because she is a woman, a Latina, or gay, she finds that she isn't offered the same opportunities as others and frequently endures microaggressions.

It wasn't until her second assignment that she came out to her boss, a two-star flag officer. Sanchez says she spoke with him because he was a fantastic leader and made her feel valued and comfortable enough to be open with him. "I would blindly walk into fire for that officer," she says, and from the way she says it you know she means it. He values her work ethnic and continues to be a mentor to her. He has taught her that there are decent people still serving that treat others with respect.

Sadly, that general has been the only boss in her ten-plus years of service that she has felt that comfortable with, and the fact that he is a flag officer is significant. Many of his peers have never worked with women in any real numbers and have never knowingly been around gay service members. "I just want people to judge me based on my work ethic and not who I go to bed with," says Sanchez. "People are still hesitant with same-sex relationships." There continue to be disparities for those in the LGBTQ community who serve, and you must be careful whom you trust, as your very safety could be in jeopardy.

It was hard for Sanchez to come out to her own parents. Her mother didn't take it well, and the fact that she is gay has certainly changed their relationship. Sanchez recalls her mother saying, "I don't care about gays as long as they are not around me." This hurt her very much. Conversely, her father came around after the initial shock. Sanchez was surprised about that, as she is from a traditional Latino family, and Latino men are not usually accepting of gays in their families. But her father said he just wanted her to be happy.

While on temporary duty to a location in Latin America, Sanchez experienced another incident of sexual harassment. She was a captain, and an Army guard major (senior to her) kept asking her out for drinks. She finally relented, but for coffee, not drinks. After this, his business texts turned into personal pursuit-type messages.

Then he upped the ante by repeatedly telling her she was beautiful and that he wanted to hang out with her, to be the man in her life. At an event out with friends, he cornered her and tried to kiss her. Sanchez told him to stop and ended up telling him she was engaged so he would leave her alone. He kept after her for a while, indicating that he was in love with her, and she just kept telling him no, that she wasn't interested. Finally, he told her he was sorry that he had been so forthcoming with her, but he had really wanted her.

Another man, an Army master sergeant on another temporary duty station, this time in South America, was more aggressive. They were working together, and the entire group would go out for drinks after a long, hard day. Sanchez says he made a comment about the women in that country being beautiful and she sort of absently agreed, just to make conversation. Then, rather brazenly, he said, "But they don't have asses like you do."

Sanchez was taken aback. Here was a senior enlisted guy talking to her like that. Without missing a beat she said to him, "You just made it really awkward, master sergeant." She says it really didn't faze him as he kept hitting on her, asking her to go with him to the hotel jacuzzi. He said he really wanted to see her in a bathing suit. Again, Sanchez just wanted to be a team player and not rock the boat. She didn't say anything more, and he kept hitting on her. She says that is just the way it is, and that she never reported any of these incidents. She didn't want to be that person who whined, who became the outlier. It was already hard enough as it was.

These two episodes were reminiscent of that first time back in the basement bar at ASBC, when she was a second lieutenant. She had been in the service for years, yet it just continued. She was repeatedly having to tell men no and fight off unwanted advances. Would it ever stop?

Sanchez speaks about being stationed in the southern part of the United States where everyone was African American but her. Instead of finding camaraderie as minorities, she says she was discriminated against for being a Latina. Sanchez says she was told that she "wasn't part of the club, wasn't their color, Black, and couldn't relate." After a time, another individual joined the team who wasn't Black either. She was Chinese. Sanchez says this enlisted troop was treated unfairly because she was different and had an accent. Even her annual evaluation was affected, despite the fact that she was a good worker. Sanchez tried to intervene and ended up getting her own evaluation downgraded.

Another time, at an event for her unit, several enlisted Latino troops asked if they could take a photo with her. They saw her as a role model, one of their own serving as an officer and leader. She agreed, but after one of the troops posted the photo on social media she was called in and accused of favoritism, showing partiality to Latino enlisted.

While deployed to Africa, she experienced additional sexual harassment from both enlisted personnel and civilian contractors. Sanchez says she kept her sexual preference private, due to the environment not being accepting and the fact that it was so easy for the men there to go rogue with sexualized behavior. Some of the women deployed there were also quite risqué. She says the culture was just crazy, almost as if no rules existed.

Sexualized banter was commonplace, especially at the gym. Everyone had to keep in shape, so Sanchez could hardly escape going to the gym. A civilian contractor started hitting on her and making very sexualized comments about her body. "You look good today girl, I like you in that position," were some of the less vulgar comments.

She avoided the gym for a while so she wouldn't have to deal with that contractor. She just wanted to work out, not get hassled, ogled, or hit on. When she did go, she would just ignore him as best she could. But he kept it up the entire six months she was there. It was very awkward and bothersome for her to go to that gym, because of him.

She also got hit on by an enlisted troop. He was in a unit with their own gym. He invited her to work out at their gym. She thought he was being kind, and that it would be a way to escape the constant come-ons from the contractor. At first he was respectful and introduced her to the team, and everything was cool. Until it wasn't.

He kept trying to hang with her, but she got that vibe from him and, when he asked her out, she said no. She knew he had ulterior motives. He began to send her selfies in workout gear, muscle type shirts, and short shorts. And he started to ask her to send him selfies in workout and bathing suits. He kept up the pursuit. She kept saying no, and eventually she went back to the other gym and endured the harassment from the contractor.

There was some safety in numbers, and the larger gym with the contractor won out in the long run. It wasn't a good situation, but she tolerated it for six months.

Sanchez recalls that liquor flowed freely in that deployed location. There was supposed to be a two-drink limit, but it was easily eluded. She says the senior enlisted ran the bar and let folks have more than the limit; it was like a racket. If you knew the right people, you could get whatever you wanted. People would trade drink limits and take turns getting wasted. The bar was like a night club. Some women wore sexy dresses. Remember this is a deployed location in Africa, not some club in Vegas. When I asked Sanchez where the leadership on this base was, she says there was no leadership, it was like a free-for-all in many ways. One night she was followed to her room, but since she made sure she always had a battle buddy with her, she was okay and told the guy following her that she didn't need his help. This deflected the situation, and he moved on.

Sanchez continues to be harassed in the workplace to this day. She is a person with integrity and character, an extremely hard worker, and a professional officer. She gets in trouble when she advocates too fiercely for her troops. When others do that, they get rewarded for their leadership. But not her. She gets told she is stepping across the line.

"As a Latina and a woman, I always felt like I had to work extra hard just to be recognized or be known," she told me. "I am constantly on guard and in competition mode. All I ever want is to be recognized for my work and the value I bring."

Sanchez says that her dream was always to serve as an officer for twenty years. She hopes she can hold out that long.

CHAPTER 13

STRONGER THAN BEFORE

Andrea Flacco[1]

I've experienced macro assaults and micro aggressions throughout my career, I tried to run from it. Now, I want to share how, like many women, I tried to ignore them, hoping I could just outrun them. However, as we know, it eventually catches up with you.

On September 11, 2001, she was in sixth grade. Her entire classroom was huddled around a television that day, watching the first attack on the U.S. homeland since Pearl Harbor. She was terrified that her best friend's mother might have been in the first plane that crashed into one of the World Trade Center towers in New York. That fear was palpable. She and her friend waited anxiously for any news. After what seemed like hours, they finally got the word that her friend's mother was not on that plane and was okay. The relief was immediate. But the sadness would stay with her.

Andrea Flacco wanted to be part of whatever the United States did to get justice for all those who died, and to help those individuals who would be involved in military efforts. She just knew that one day she was going to serve in the military. It didn't matter that no one in her immediate family

---

1 Andrea Flacco is a pseudonym for this active-duty sailor.

183

had served, or that she had absolutely no idea what the military was about. She was determined to do something.

The 9/11 attack became the catalyst for serving her country. More than twenty years have passed, but she remembers it like it was yesterday. She recalls watching events unfold over the following weeks and months, U.S. troops headed first to Afghanistan then to Iraq. "I remember thinking, 'I want to be part of this someday,'" she says. She started going to military-themed summer camps, to learn as much as she could about the military.

As of 2022, Andrea is a serving active-duty lieutenant (O-3) in the Navy, stationed on the East Coast. She's served on both coasts of the United States, on an island in Micronesia, on a carrier, deployed underway at sea, in harm's way at a base on the ground in Afghanistan, and as part of a huge effort to combat the coronavirus on a floating naval hospital. To say that she has accomplished much in her nine-plus years of military service to date would be an understatement. And she isn't done serving yet.

Andrea grew up in Indianapolis. She has two siblings and is the middle child. Her homelife included some physical, emotional, and verbal abuse. As a young child, when she would have a nightmare, her mother would slap her and tell her to get over it. Andrea says that true empathy and concern were not found in her mother's behavior. Her father was much more compassionate, which helped somewhat to balance out her upbringing. Making things that much more confusing for Andrea was when her mother would say negative things about her father and his side of the family, telling her that her father hated her and wasn't a good person. In fact, she recollects her mother telling her that living in an environment that entailed abusive behavior like hitting, yelling, and walking on eggshells was equated to how much she was loved.

What was hardest for young Andrea to experience was when her mother would hug her and say she loved her, then turn around and say terrible things or hit her. Andrea grew up thinking that this behavior meant her mother loved her. This abusive homelife was her reality and became normal to her. "It took a long time to untangle the truth and unpack all the abusive behavior," she says. "Pain and hurt doesn't equal love."

Even a tumultuous homelife and living with constant uncertainty and fear didn't prevent Andrea from pouring herself into sports and academics. Perhaps it even helped propel her into achieving excellence, as she did quite well in both. A competitive swimmer in her early years and throughout high school, she played additional sports, many of them considered male-dominated, like hockey, baseball, karate, and football. She grew up competing athletically around boys. Later in life she took on MMA (mixed martial arts), which is also a heavily male-dominated sport. She was an overachiever and a thrill seeker with her extracurriculars and athletic pursuits. She parlayed dedication and merit into earning a scholarship right out of high school.

She garnered a highly competitive, sought-after Naval ROTC scholarship, a fully paid four-year education culminating in a bachelor of science degree and ultimately becoming a registered nurse. Of course, it came with a commitment to serve her country. That didn't dismay her, as she was driven, and her athletic experience would translate easily into the rigors of being a full-time college student and being in NROTC. Those o'dark thirty physical training sessions were not going to be a problem for Andrea. She attended a university in Florida with a Naval ROTC program, far from Indiana.

The rigid school schedule kept her focused, but she says her first day of NROTC was a huge culture shock. She had been told to wear something nice. To Andrea, that meant a skirt and flipflops. They were all made to run, up and down stairwells. Welcome to ROTC. They weren't playing; the physical conditioning began immediately. She laughingly remembers being teased for showing up like that.

But she took to the NROTC structure and its disciplined regimen quite well. The NROTC unit was half Navy and half Marines, and very people-focused. What Andrea loved about her experience was that it "helped form the basis of what I wanted to accomplish as a leader," she says. "There was always someone who was there to help me, guide me, and keep me on track."

Andrea recalls a time in NROTC when all the midshipmen toured a ship, and one of the deck sailors looked up at her, called her by name and said, "Flacco, we've heard about you." She had just gotten aboard the ship, no one knew her except her fellow midshipmen, but word had already spread that there was a woman in the touring group. "It was a good warning for me, that everyone is watching your every move as a woman," she says. Years later, serving, everyone did watch her and knew her every move aboard the ship. She was under unbelievable scrutiny. "It was like being constantly under a microscope and very exhausting," she recalls.

The NROTC environment taught her to put people first. She was a sponge soaking up everything the prior service midshipmen, enlisted and officer cadre, put out. She had a significant leadership role her senior year as a company commander. She graduated from college cum laude, and with a solid start on what leadership could look like once she went active duty.

But her college time wasn't always happy. She became involved in an extremely toxic relationship with a man she had dated as a teenager, but this time it took a much darker turn.

It wasn't always an abusive relationship. There were times when he was gentle and kind. She had met him when she was 15 and he was 21. Most parents of a 15-year-old daughter would try to steer their daughter away from getting involved with such an older man. Andrea says that in fact, her mother approved her dating him. After a few weeks, Andrea came to the realization on her own that it just wasn't right, there was something wrong about dating such an older guy. After all, she was a freshman in high school.

Later, as a senior, she began to think she could date him again. She was a bit older and more mature. They dated for about a month, then she broke it off. She was quite busy in her senior year with swimming and chasing scholarships for college, and he had joined the military and departed for boot camp.

She got her scholarship, and he ended up deploying. Later, while attending college and with her NROTC commitments, her days and evenings were quite busy. However, she became aware of how immature some of her male fellow college students were and decided to give her older former boyfriend a call.

Turns out he was dating someone else at the time, but he called her back several weeks later. He informed her that he had broken up with the other girl and asked her if she wanted to start dating again. Now she was a sophomore in college, not the young girl he might have remembered. The first few weeks were good, and he was so kind to her. "I even thought he might be the one," she told me. She told him that she loved him deeply.

But she was conflicted about having sex before marriage, as she was deeply Catholic. She spoke with her mother about it, and her mother encouraged her to start taking birth control. However, she still felt deeply conflicted between her relationship and her faith.

When she brought these concerns to her boyfriend, his response shocked her: "If you don't have sex with me, I will find another way to take my anger out on you." Looking back now, Andrea can say that there certainly were red flags all around the relationship. But back then she continued to make excuses for him. She says he was angry a lot after returning from his deployment to Iraq and depressed. "All he wanted to do was have sex and sleep. He was so very angry." Still, she made excuses for him.

Andrea was sexually inexperienced, and he was her first partner. After growing up in an environment with both physical, emotional, and verbal abuse, she believed that she had chosen the relationship so she must deserve what was happening to her.

So, when he took what he wanted from her, she just froze. During and after the encounters, she just lay there crying. Each time she lay there concentrating on the details in the room, so she wouldn't be in the moment actually experiencing his forcefully assaulting her. Andrea recalls that, during what she would take years to recognize as the rapes, her mind left her body and it was like it was happening to someone else, not to her. She remembers "feeling trapped and concentrating on the details in the room, like the bedspread, pictures on the walls, the colors purple and green." Concentrating on everything but what was happening to her allowed her somehow to escape what was occurring. During the assaults, her boyfriend saw her tears and then watched her sob afterwards. According to Andrea, he knew that after each incident she was in the bathroom crying and scrubbing herself clean, but he never stopped his behavior.

"I was so used to being hurt by the people who loved me," Andrea says sadly. At age 20, after three months of this, she finally opened up to a friend, and that person told her that what was happening to her was not okay. This was the first time Andrea had ever heard those words. "I'm lucky that finally

I confided in the right person, who first told me that I never deserved to be treated like that and that I should get out of that relationship," she says.

She was still scared of her boyfriend, but her friend gave her the courage she needed to tell him that she couldn't do it anymore. She broke it off for good this time, as she could not see herself married to someone that could hurt her in the way he had.

When she told her mother about the breakup, her mother got angry and asked her, "What did you do to him?"

"I told him I didn't want to have sex, and he threatened to hurt me and made me," she told her mother. Her mother replied, "I unfriended him on Facebook, but I hope you know that this feels like I am losing a son." To Andrea, her mother didn't seem concerned for her wellbeing or what she had been through. It was very traumatic, and then for her mother not even to inquire about her physical or emotional condition relayed to Andrea the untrue belief that her trauma was not important and that she didn't deserve sympathy, empathy, or help.

In fact, Andrea believes firmly: "I think if we really want to change rape culture and sexual assault mindset, it needs to start with mothers and fathers at home and their little girls." She says that she froze because that is what she had done throughout her life, to survive physical, emotional, and verbal abuse growing up. "If you freeze, you can survive." Fighting and trying to run away had not gone well for her in the past, and she wanted to live.

And live she did. She says the best part of being in the military was the people she served with. She made some great friends. "I found people of like mind, carpe diem type people, who go out and take more risks and live a little more extreme lifestyles, a more robust life," she told me.

Andrea was not intimidated when she entered active duty. Her prior experience in male-dominated sports and in NROTC helped prepare her to don the uniform. In fact, she says her father used to joke that he wasn't worried about her, since she led her team in penalties in hockey for three years running.

Since she joined the Navy as a registered nurse and an officer, she had more than just military culture and rank to deal with. She quickly learned about the medical hierarchy: doctors, residents, nurses, attending physicians. She felt four years in NROTC had given her a head start on the military culture and rank structure, but she had to learn quickly about the medical hierarchy's structure and language. There were challenges in learning both, and knowing when one might have had priority in a particular setting.

"It was an interesting change going from medicine, where there are more women, then going to certain commands, where the number of women was extremely small," says Andrea. There were times she was the only nurse on board a ship, and one of very few women. It was the same in Afghanistan.

Andrea recalls one occasion when she first arrived at a new unit after she had just returned from her tour in Afghanistan. The commanding officer was hosting a welcome-to-the-unit meeting with the new personnel, eight men and two women. "I specifically remember the commander asking all the males about their combat deployment experiences, but not asking the two women." She had just completed her deployment and couldn't believe that the commander would just skip over her like that. She wasn't asked about her Afghanistan deployment or about her career or any of her experiences. It was almost as if she and the other woman weren't even in the room. The commander went on to talk about how he was glad he had sons and not daughters, how he had put them in hockey, and that he didn't know what he would have done with girls. Andrea was stunned. She had played hockey for seven years!

Thinking back on that situation she says, "I really wished that I had had the foresight and the ability to correct him at that point. I wished I had spoken up." This left a lasting impression on her and only added to her sense that she really wasn't welcome in that unit. She found it so egregious that the commander was so explicit in allowing his own biases to show. She recalls feeling that her military contributions were discounted and that this type of behavior makes it that much harder for her and other women to be taken seriously.

"It was rough to have it be assumed that I didn't know how to play in a man's world," she says. She participated in MMA, hockey, and football, and recalls that a lot of the friends she spent time with in these activities were men. She wasn't a lightweight; she certainly pulled her own weight in and out of the military.

In time, Andrea learned how to call people out when they made sexist or sexualized comments or acted inappropriately in her presence. Over the years she worked with some very strong women who were supportive. She recalls an incident where a photo of the medical unit had been taken while on a port call, depicting all the personnel in the unit, men and women. Two wives of two of the male officers in the unit saw the photo, inquired as to who Andrea was, and alleged that she was sleeping around with one of their husbands. The women sent a letter with the allegation to the XO and the JAG in the unit, and an investigation was conducted. The allegations were not substantiated.

However, Andrea had to go through this entire sordid ordeal, where her character was questioned. Others in the medical unit were interviewed. She even had to contact her parents and her boyfriend to inform them of what was going on, in case the whole thing got blown up even further with media. "It made me angry, that instead of my legal department pursuing these people for slander and libel, they just didn't do anything," she says.

She was grateful that her own department and leadership handled it professionally, but she wonders about other junior officers and enlisted out there who would not get the support she did. "This type of behavior scares me for the junior women serving, that don't have the same ability to stand up for themselves," she says. "I'm fearful for them, their reputation and career opportunities. Some of them are forced out of the service, especially if they don't play the game. They can be impacted professionally and personally." Andrea knows from personal experience just how such an ordeal can impact one's psyche and reputation.

"I've experienced macro assaults and micro aggressions throughout my career, I tried to run from it," she asserts. "Now I want to share how, like many women, I tried to ignore them, hoping I could just outrun them. However, as we know, it eventually catches up with you."

She describes a sexual assault that occurred with a Marine officer, someone she had known for several years and thought of as a friend. They had attended college together and been midshipmen in the same NROTC program. She had known him for five or six years and trusted him. They ended up in the same part of the country once he completed officer candidate school.

According to Andrea they met for dinner, and she consumed a cocktail and a glass of wine. He had one beer. When it was time to leave, she didn't feel comfortable driving, as she had just come off a month-long no-alcohol diet and felt a little bit off. She ended up staying at his place and didn't initially stay on the couch since he had roommates, so she stayed in his room. She was wearing a sweater dress and it was very hot, so she took it off but kept on her underwear, which was basically like a bikini bathing suit.

Andrea says she fell asleep and awoke to him on top of her, kissing and groping her and more. She kept saying to him, "Please don't, please don't do this, it will change everything," and him replying, "It will be fine." She describes this incident as her being in sort of a fog, like having an out of body experience, as she could see his back on top of her.

When the fog lifted and she realized what had happened, she put on her dress and went to sleep on the couch, disregarding the roommates at this point as she was very distraught and traumatized. She describes her memories of this incident as being like a dreamscape. She felt totally betrayed by someone who had been a friend and a fellow military officer. The betrayal by a brother in arms hurt her deeply.

Andrea recalls that she didn't report the sexual assault or press charges, as she knew due to alcohol being involved that it would impact her career. Plus, she believed that her having taken off her own dress would have been used against her, along with all her past relationships. She knew her reputation would be affected. She did confide in one person, and she remembers clearly that person saying, "Have you thought about how this will affect his career?"

The double standard that exists in these types of situations is hard to accept. "This is always looked at from the male perspective, never the woman's," says Andrea. "They don't see it as a crime. Rape culture needs to change. The laws need to be changed, along with how survivors are dealt with."

All of Andrea's past incidents of sexual assault, rape, sexual harassment, and sexism, to include her childhood trauma, all came crashing down on her while serving aboard ship upon returning from Afghanistan. She had outrun it as long as she could, but could no longer compartmentalize. She couldn't sleep, was working really long days, under stress, not eating properly or working out as she typically did.

She began to have dreams of her past sexual assaults and childhood abuse. They included seeing past assaults over and over again and reliving the assaults. Like some victims of extreme abuse, her brain started to plug in ways to escape the pain, including witnessing her own death. She couldn't escape the past traumas; they continued to invade her thoughts, whether she was awake or asleep. "I was physically and mentally exhausted," she says. "My brain was so tired. My resilience wasn't there."

She needed help. Fortunately, one of her shipmates was a licensed marriage and family counselor and started to speak with her. Andrea had sought out therapy years ago earlier, off the books so to speak, with civilian providers, and the military knew nothing of it. She was afraid that the Navy would use it against her and didn't want her deployability or her clearance affected.

The counselor felt that staying on board the ship was not a good idea or a place where Andrea could get the help she needed. The leadership on board all rallied around to ensure she could get off the ship to get the help she needed. Not an easy task, to get someone off the ship and find a replacement. But that is exactly what happened.

"They were all so great, took care of me, got me to the right place for help," she told me. "I'm very grateful for how it worked out for me." She landed in an intensive outpatient program and for the first time got the support she so desperately needed. She faced her demons.

The psychologist Andrea saw told her that she wasn't crazy, that her brain was trying to protect her, especially since she had been so exhausted. The opstempo serving in a deployed combat location like Afghanistan is unrelenting and then returning to a ship, going underway, preparing to deploy again, combined with all her built-in stressors from trauma, was all too much.

"I didn't want to emulate the example I had growing up," she reflects. "I didn't know what was normal, what was acceptable, how to 'adult' in a healthy way, just didn't want to live like I was raised." It was important that she no longer had to conceal either the fact that she had experienced such devastating trauma or that she had sought out help for it. This allowed her to concentrate on getting better. The right medications and therapy, and the ability to focus on her mental wellbeing, allowed her to progress in healing.

She joined an all-women sexual assault group through one of the military hospital's programs and found it really helped her. She saw that MST affects people for years, and that she wasn't alone in what had happened to her or how she thought about it. She began to unpack what had happened to her, along with her own reactions and those of others.

Not all reactions to her trauma were helpful, and in fact some were downright harmful. When one tells others about having been assaulted or raped, that initial feedback is so very important to the person painfully disclosing what they have gone through. "In both of my rape cases, they discounted the incidents," Andrea says. "It taught me that the pain and suffering I underwent wasn't important." Andrea wants people to understand just how critical the initial response to an MST survivor really is.

I first met Andrea after a *VFW Magazine* article about my MST experiences was published in June/July 2021.[2] She read the piece and immediately felt she had to reach out to me. She sent me the following message:

> First of all, thank you for [your] years of service, not only to our country, but to the women (like me) who came into the military after you. I read the VFW article about you breaking your silence after the Vanessa Guillén case. I'd like to tell my story and help this cause.

This took tremendous courage, because she was active duty, and to speak out would come at some risk. I already had another active-duty individual as part of the book, and I informed Andrea that I would not reveal the identities of those still serving. Initially she wanted me to, but after some discussion she understood why I was so adamant about concealing her identity.

Andrea has more mettle than many of the people I served in combat with. To reveal the deeply personal experiences she had growing up, while

---

2 Janie Dyhouse, *VFW Magazine*, June/July 2021, pp. 32-33, http://digitaledition. qwinc.com/publication/?m=3914&i=704409&p=34&ver=html5.

in college, and in the military, these painful traumas say so much about her character. She wants to make a difference, try to change the culture within the military, and help those junior to her, so they are treated with much more respect and sensitivity than she was.

She states firmly: "With lots of work, self-love and forgiveness of the things you cannot control, it is possible to recover and come out on the other side different, but also stronger than you were before." Indeed, she is a strong woman warrior. I am grateful for her strength. Glad she is in the Navy standing watch for us, willing to draw attention to MST, even if it means that she is now on the front lines, sharing her story to help the women and men who are affected.

CHAPTER 14

#IAmVanessaGuillen

Karina Lopez

I loved my first assignment. It was really great, the people were very supportive in a variety of ways. But my second assignment was a nightmare. I experienced multiple occasions of MST and, when I tried to speak up, was silenced, never taken seriously.

Fort Hood. Two words that dredge up so much raw emotion and pain, as it has been the site for so many tragedies over the years. In 2020 alone, the Texas base saw 25 deaths by murder, suicide, and accidents, along with multiple incidents of sexual assault and sexual harassment. Many soldiers and their families have suffered. The demand for the Army to do something reached a crescendo following the disappearance and horrific murder of Vanessa Guillén in April 2020. Joining the Guillén family in the early search for Vanessa, and in demanding an investigation into what happened, were legislators, advocacy groups and thousands of individuals.[1]

---

1 See "US Army fires Ft Hood officers and order policy shift following 25 deaths," *The Guardian*, December 9, 2020, https://www.theguardian.com/us-news/2020/dec/09/fort-hood-army-base-officers-fired-deaths-sexual-assault.

One of those individuals was another young Latina, an Army soldier who had been stationed at Fort Hood just a month before Vanessa disappeared in April 2020. The name of the Army base brings up painful memories for her of being sexually assaulted and harassed, and of the retaliation she encountered after reporting what happened to her.

Karina Lopez related to Vanessa on multiple levels. Both were young Latinas serving in the Army. And both had been sexually harassed at Fort Hood. The harassment never abated for Karina, and in fact escalated until it became unbearable. She was also sexually assaulted there. She did report the incidents. It did not go well. She ended up leaving the service in March 2020 at age 23 with an honorable discharge. She had had enough.

As a recently separated soldier, a DoD whistleblower, MST survivor, and now veteran, Karina began advocating for Vanessa in an intentional way via social media just after the disappearance was reported. She was desperate to help find the missing soldier. She knew just how toxic Vanessa's unit was, and she started talking to anyone she could to bring attention to the missing soldier. Karina says no one would listen, so in May 2020 she wrote a letter to Vanessa on social media, opening up about her own sexual assault and sexual harassment at Fort Hood and how after reporting everything just got worse, as if she were being retraumatized over and over again.

Then, on June 19, Karina created the #IAmVanessaGuillen hashtag to help bring awareness to sexual assault and sexual harassment, to spur action to find Vanessa and to highlight injustice within the military. What happened next astonished even Karina herself. It went viral! Military and veteran women and men everywhere started sharing their stories of military sexual trauma on social and other media. This started an avalanche of powerful voices sharing their MST experiences. "When I saw Vanessa's story, then created the hashtag and it went viral, the first five responses came from friends of mine, people I had known," she remembers. "A wild time of emotions. It broke me. People needed to see this."

Vanessa's remains were discovered on June 30, 2020, miles from Fort Hood. This did not stop the steady stream of voices from telling their stories. It was as if the floodgates had opened, and there was no stopping the force of the waters coming through. Military members and veterans who had never shared before were speaking out loudly, intensely, and painfully, joining the voices of those who had been crying out for years.

Now, with the finality of her murder, the cries for justice began screaming out forcefully and persistently, and they continue to this day. There seemed to be no stopping the movement for change and for justice. And not just for Vanessa, but for so many others who have been assaulted, harassed, raped, or murdered. The avalanche continued to grow and build.

All these collective voices helped compel the Army to act, and an Independent Review Committee was finally assembled to investigate the situation at Fort Hood surrounding Vanessa's murder and the climate regarding sexual harassment. The committee's report was published on November 6, 2020.[2]

The report brought into the harsh light of day for all to see many skeletons from Fort Hood's closet. Nine findings were specified, along with seventy recommendations. Finding #2 states: "There Is Strong Evidence That Incidents Of Sexual Assault And Sexual Harassment At Fort Hood Are Significantly Underreported." Finding #9 states: "The Command Climate At Fort Hood Has Been Permissive Of Sexual Harassment/Sexual Assault."

Fort Hood's leadership failures impacted many, and Karina was one of them. Her experiences at the Army base have caused much harm to the young Latina. The system designed to protect her not only allowed an environment of permissiveness to exist surrounding sexual assault and sexual harassment, but actually ended up harming her again once she reported the incidents. "The amount of threats tripled, the harassment was unbearable, and my workplace was as hostile as it could get, and nothing was done to help me," Karina told me.

Just who is Karina Lopez? How could a 23-year-old Latina make such a bold impact and galvanize what some are calling the military's #metoo movement? First and foremost, she is a fighter, one tough Latina. Second, she demands justice for herself and many others. She is also courageous

---

2 "Report of the Ft Hood Independent Review Committee," November 6, 2020, Executive summary, pg iii of ix, https://www.army.mil/e2/downloads/rv7/forthoodreview/2020-12-03_FHIRC_report_redacted.pdf.

enough to tell her own story and speak up calling for changes. She is #IAmVanessaGuillen.

Her story started long before Fort Hood, with a young girl who wanted to serve her country, continuing traditions that many in her family had established. Karina is an Afro-Latina and very proud of her Dominican and Puerto Rican heritage. She was born in New York but grew up in North Carolina. She comes from a long line of those who served in the military, starting with her great-grandfather and her grandfather, and including many extended family members of both sexes.

Although her mother didn't serve in the military, she was in law enforcement. It seemed that most of Karina's family wore a uniform of some kind. Putting others first was something this family did instinctively. Karina remembers at a young age waiting for her aunt to come in from the Navy ship she served on. She just knew that the military would be in her future.

Karina has five siblings and several step siblings, and they are all part of a very large and loving family. She worked for a few years after high school but saw herself serving. Once her mother fell ill, she joined so she could assist the family in a variety of ways. She wanted to be a paralegal in the Air Force, but the waiting list was too long and she was underweight. She wanted to get into the military quickly and have a short advanced technical training slot. She ended up in the Army, because it was the quickest way to get in.

Her mother didn't want her to join, but her grandfather was super proud. The family supported her, even if they were concerned about her serving. They gave her advice and tried to explain to her the realities of serving, as a woman and a minority. Several of the women who had served pointed out the Lavina Johnson case to her. Johnson allegedly committed suicide in Iraq, but her family believes she was beaten, raped, and murdered. The case remains categorized by the Army as a suicide.[3]

Karina's family discussed sexual violence with her and told her always to have a battle buddy. "I was so naïve," she says, looking back. She really had no idea of how bad it could really get, and it started immediately at boot camp. Even though she didn't focus on the men, they focused on her.

At basic training, she was constantly told she was a distraction for the

---

3 See https://www.protectourdefenders.com/the-johnson-family-story/.

men. "In the barracks, the guys talked about how cute, gorgeous I was," she recalls. She remembers getting that certain kind of look that some women are all too familiar with from the drill sergeant. "If you were pretty, you got duties with that specific drill sergeant, who gave you those looks, and got assigned duties that were more favorable," she says. "You were their eye candy." She clearly witnessed favoritism play out at basic. However, at the time she normalized this behavior and rationalized it, as her being appreciated for her hard work.

Physical training wasn't a problem for Karina. "I always pushed myself and did more than required for push-ups and run times, but they would only talk about my looks." Her physical fitness was largely due to her mother. Laughingly, she remembers that her mother made them all do pushups growing up. In a softer tone, she says, "Basic made me feel so close to my mom, as I now understood why her feet would hurt." Her mother wore boots all day, pulling double shifts in law enforcement.

After basic, it was on to AIT (advanced individual training) for tech school to learn about her career field, which was 25U, signal support systems specialist. Basically like an IT position that dealt with communication equipment, radios and computers. The AIT experience included lots of sexualized comments and harassment. Karina remembers an instructor who was sleeping with trainees. She says this same instructor ogled and leered at her.

There were incidents at AIT that truly affected Karina. One in particular was egregious. In the barracks living area, there were curtains that allowed some semblance of privacy. However, Karina's curtains were removed by her leadership. She says that a sergeant said to her, "We took away your curtain because you don't tell anyone when you get out of the shower so we can take a peek." She and her fellow women ended up putting sheets throughout the living area, and eventually her curtain was returned. Karina says juvenile and degrading stuff like this happened quite a bit, was SOP, standard operating procedure. This particular sergeant was known for this type of behavior.

After AIT, it was on to Korea. There she found the traditional values of the military that she had sought. She thought that she had found somewhat of a family in her fellow soldiers, especially being overseas and at her first duty location. Fortunately, she encountered great women role models in leadership in Korea. In fact, one stood up for her when a sexual harassment incident occurred.

At the time, she had been assigned to a medevac unit and was on a twelve-hour work schedule. The team lived above their work office area, in a co-ed living environment. Karina never had any problems until the night one of her male coworkers cornered her in the kitchen space and began telling her how great she looked in yoga pants, even better after working out. According to Karina, he started to ask for sexual favors. "I felt trapped," she told me. "He was blocking the doorway. I remember just standing there, and him going on and on with sexualized comments."

A fellow woman, a sergeant Karina confided in, told her to stand up for herself and instructed her on what to say to him. So Karina told him not to speak to her again, not to disrespect her like that. He was removed from the company, and she felt not only validated in having spoken up but comforted by how her unit had handled it. "It was so refreshing to have the unit's support," she recalls. She felt empowered in Korea and believed she was strong, like her mother.

That sense of empowerment would be degraded at her second duty location, where she did not get the support or respect she needed. Fort Hood was the antithesis of Korea in that respect. The environment was not a supportive family type one, but one almost of lawlessness, where individuals acted on their own with no real adult supervision.

"I loved my first assignment," Karina told me. "It was really great, the people were very supportive in a variety of ways. But my second assignment was a nightmare. I experienced multiple occasions of MST and, when I tried to speak up, was silenced, never taken seriously."

It didn't start out that bad, but quickly developed into a situation where Karina states: "I have been threatened, belittled, humiliated, intimidated, mentally and emotionally abused by those same people who were supposed to teach me and lead me to be a great soldier."

Karina had injured her arm in Korea, so she showed up to Fort Hood and was quickly judged as inferior and teased. Her body wasn't as strong as it used to be, as she had suffered nerve damage in her injured arm. She tried not to let it get to her, but the harassment grew negative and dark. She powered through, even completed combat training with a brace on her injured arm. "They made me feel like dirt, worthless, and they exploited every weakness," she says. She had been a high-speed soldier prior to this and had much difficulty dealing with her injury.

In 2018, she intervened in an incident to protect another woman. Once safely home she herself was sexually assaulted in her room. "This made me feel less than human," she says. According to Karina, the perpetrator was an E-5, and she was an E-4. He was someone from her own unit. She remembers that he used her injury against her, as he focused on holding down other parts of her body. She recalls that he groped her, sexually assaulted her, and bit her on the thigh. Karina says she fought and punched him in the face as hard as she could. She connected, cutting his eye, and later his black eye was evident for all to see.

The next morning in formation, Karina said he tried to wear sunglasses, but Karina recalls that his fellow soldiers saw his black eye and messed-up face and started shouting at him, "Did you finally meet the only girl that told you no?"

Karina clearly remembers her perpetrator telling her that if she spoke up about what happened, she would be "the next body they would find in the woods." The harassment continued and increased. She recollects that at night this sergeant and his friends would throw glass bottles against her window. The bottles would smash and break against the window and walls. Karina says it was nerve-wracking and intimidating. Making matters worse was that one of her roommates was friends with him.

Karina says that this roommate would invite her perpetrator and his friends into their room. They would just hang in their common space. She believes that they were just increasing their intimidation tactics. Karina says she was even told not to go to behavioral health, that it would affect her career, and that she was bribed with a better position on a deployment. They just didn't want her to report the sexual assault.

This began to wear on her, day after day, night after night. She went without sleeping or eating. Her friends were scared to leave her alone and would take turns being there when she showered, to ensure no one approached her. Karina says she couldn't even do her laundry at night, because her perpetrator's room was on the first floor near the laundry. Karina's room was on the second floor.

After several days of this constant harassment and fear, Karina indicates she was put on staff duty, but she was shaking and was so sleep deprived that the staff duty sergeant told her chain of command that she needed to get some help. She finally was able to see a psychiatrist and was placed on several medications, which just made it worse, as she says she didn't feel like herself.

It was at this very low point that she finally decided to report her roommate and the bottle throwing. Karina says that her roommate was involved in unsavory activities. What happened? Karina was moved out of the unit.

She goes to another unit, finds out that some of the sergeants from her previous unit were friends with her perpetrator. It appeared the harassers were following her. Karina felt like she couldn't do anything right. She believes that someone in the new unit leaked information about the meds she was on, because she ended up getting harassed about that. She found herself right back in the same type of hostile environment she had just left.

It just kept getting worse and, according to Karina, one of the enlisted leaders, a sergeant and a woman, told her, "Go use your body language to get what we need." Karina says she felt like this NCO was "pimping her out to male soldiers." Harassing remarks like, "Lopez likes it when you talk to her rough," were just part of the abuse she was under daily.

Karina recalls that at one point she was pinned up against a wall and her hair was pulled. She states that men would say they were "way too hard to stand up around her," meaning that they had erections. She states that even one senior enlisted got in on the harassment; he would bang on the table and degrade her. She didn't feel safe on the base at all. Repeated jokes about her body, especially her butt, and sexualized comments about her mother became commonplace. She says that if she spoke up, she would be put on the worst details.

"Every time I would try to go to the IG, they would hold something over my head saying they would bring up charges against me," she asserts. She says they kept up a war of harassment and administrative admonishments against her. In fact, she recalls that they racked up several counselings so they could eventually demote her. She says her punishment never matched anyone else's. An example was the excessive negative counselings she received. It was almost as if they were trying to build a case with repeated allegations against her. She was in fact demoted. She says they went so far as to inform her mother that it could be worse.

"I became this sheltered, isolated, anxious, depressed, and suicidal individual who just wanted to run home to Mom," Karina says. The toxic workplace, the constant harassment, the retaliation was so over the top. According to Karina, they twisted and manipulated all to show that she was the manipulator and the instigator, and that everything that occurred was her fault.

Karina says that for two years after she reported the MST, her allegations of sexual assault and sexual harassment were not taken seriously. The case had been closed. After she released the letter to Vanessa and the hashtag on social media, she was called and told that they now believed her, but that they couldn't locate the perpetrator. Karina throws the BS flag on that. After all, he was a sergeant in the Army and had been in her own unit. Shouldn't be that hard to locate.

All this took its toll and Karina was in fact suicidal by this point. According to Karina, she was labeled as a suicide risk but was never placed on suicide watch. Her mother, acting on Karina's behalf, took the allegations of MST outside of her chain of command and contacted the command sergeant major. He helped her, and she was assigned a victim advocate. However, one time she was chased in the parking lot and had to hide under a car until her victim advocate could come out to help her. The harassment and threatening behavior continued the entire time she was at Fort Hood. Still concerned about Karina, her mother contacted a senator's office.

Enough was enough, her physical and mental wellbeing were at stake. She filed the IG complaint of unfair treatment and hostile work environment and added in a whistleblower complaint for retaliation. Finally, her case would be properly investigated. There were so many leadership failures in her situation, says Karina. There were times when people could have helped her but chose not to, either looking the other way, covering it up, or joining in on all the harassment and retaliation.

Karina's case is not yet resolved, but now she has powerful allies like Protect Our Defenders (POD), an advocacy group that fights for and assists MST survivors. You can read more about them in Chapter 15. Karina says she came out of the military fighting. She serves with POD as an advocate for other MST survivors, and she has served on panels and engagements with other organizations and advocacy groups.

Advocacy groups working on the prevention of sexual assault and sexual harassment began to contact her. They told her, "You did a big thing, what no one else has been able to do. Karina, you started a movement." She and her mother have done interviews together, to keep up the momentum for justice and change.

"I am so glad I spoke up," Karina told me. "Some of my family didn't know, so this past year has been dedicated to healing. Just wait, next year I will be a force to be reckoned with!" She already is a force to be reckoned with, wiser beyond her years and matured by traumatic experiences.

And many others have noticed as well. She has done work with Minority Veterans of America as a research and policy analyst. She attends college on-line and is pursuing higher education. She is helping others who have been assaulted or harassed. She knows firsthand how traumatic the experiences can be, and she offers insight gleaned from her own abuse.

The Latino media giant Univision noticed Karina, and they are now actively working with her as the primary focus of a documentary about MST and Latinas. I've had the privilege of collaborating with Univision on the documentary, and I know that it will be a powerful story detailing Karina's experiences and the advocacy she is doing now to help others.

Karina is indeed a fighter, and she is fighting to regain her sense of safety and security when around others, especially military or veteran men. In fact, her mentor in college is a male Navy veteran. Little by little she is working on finding a new normal, one that is hers post-sexual assault and sexual harassment, post the military.

She is a deeply spiritual individual and seeks holistic ways to heal. She has the support of her family and the thousands of sisters and brothers who have her to thank for the #IAmVanessaGuillen movement.

The Department of Defense is on the cusp of real change, with the passage of the NDAA in December 2021 which includes the I Am Vanessa Guillén Act, making sexual harassment a crime for the first time in military history and taking sexual assault and sexual harassment crimes out of the military chain of command. The future is brighter for MST survivors, thanks to Karina's courage and sacrifices. Her sheer will to do something when a fellow young Latina soldier went missing and was later found murdered woke up the country and gave military members and veterans an avenue to speak up and be heard.

Getting Help

CHAPTER 15

SUPPORT AND ADVOCACY FOR MST SURVIVORS

You've learned about the lived experiences of several veteran and active-duty individuals who experienced military sexual trauma. This chapter will briefly discuss Protect our Defenders (POD), a nonprofit solely dedicated to ending injustices within the military regarding sexual violence, survivor retaliation, misogyny, sexual prejudice, and racism. I consider them to be a major player on the MST battlefield.

Military sexual trauma is a complex issue, and there are many organizations and resources available to those who have endured it and their supporters. Please refer to Appendix I for a more exhaustive list of resources. One must explore the best option available for one's own unique situation.

Protect Our Defenders was founded in 2011 by Nancy Parrish, who serves as its chief executive officer. According to POD's president, retired Air Force colonel and former chief prosecutor Don Christensen, for several years prior to founding POD, Parrish's friend U.S. Rep. Jackie Speier had been gathering the stories of military members who were survivors of sexual assault. Rep. Speier started sharing their stories by reading them on the floor of the House of Representatives and urged Parrish to start an organization to fight for the survivors.

Over the years, POD has evolved into an organization that does much more than share stories. Through research, public education, policy, legislative efforts, and pro bono legal support, they are making an impact assisting military members and veterans in moving forward with seeking justice.

POD understood years ago that the military commanders were failing the many MST survivors they spoke with, and it wanted to stand in the gap to help in two major actionable ways: by getting survivor stories out there, and by helping reform the actual process that survivors go through in the military as they seek support, treatment, and justice.

Christensen's first interaction with POD was while he was still active duty as a judge advocate general (JAG) in the Air Force. He had seen over the years how commanders dealt with sexual assault and sexual harassment cases, and in his mind the needs of the survivors were not being intentionally considered in a holistic way. He saw this firsthand during a particular sexual assault case in which, after a conviction was won, it was overturned by the military convening authority in the chain of command. "I was disgusted that the Air Force response was to protect the offender and not aid the victim," he says.

He then advised the victim in the case to reach out to POD for support. The victim did just that, then asked Christensen to talk with Parrish. It was 2013 and Parrish informed Christensen that they were on the same side, that of justice and survivor support. It didn't matter that he was on active duty. After some thought, just 18 months later Christensen retired from the Air Force and began to work with POD on a full-time basis, bringing with him the very insight that they needed to make real headway towards military justice reform.

With Christensen on board, POD was now better suited to tackle the reform part of their mission. "I brought subject matter expertise and the knowledge to point out existing problems in the military justice system," he says. Christensen has collaborated with legislators in various efforts to reform the military justice system and played a major role in advocating for the changes that were passed in the 2021 National Defense Authorization Act (NDAA). These included the I Am Vanessa Guillén Act provisions, one of which was to establish sexual harassment as a crime under the Uniform Code of Military Justice.

Only recently has POD been able to meet with Secretary of Defense Lloyd J. Austin III. Along with several other advocacy groups, POD met with Secretary Austin on at least three occasions to discuss sexual assault, sexual harassment, and recommendations for military justice reforms. Christensen says that POD had never met with any prior administration's senior military leadership, and this was a huge step in moving forward toward progress. Both President Biden and Secretary Austin have spoken up about ending the scourge of sexual assault within the military.

Christensen says he maintains a good relationship with the Department of Veterans Affairs and in fact gives them a lot of credit, more than most survivors do, for trying to improve services, benefit processing, and care for survivors. The VA has been making inroads in the treatment of MST and has placed military sexual trauma coordinators in most regional medical centers.

How exactly does POD help combat MST? First and foremost, says Christensen, it highlights the problem, followed by proposing legislative fixes, advocacy efforts, pointing out a whole host of areas that need reform within the military justice system, and highlighting how the institutions involved can better provide information to survivors.

More specifically, POD directly supports MST survivors, by providing them a safe space to share their experiences with POD staff and advocates, assists them to tell their stories with the media, the public, legislators, and those who can amplify their voices. POD also provides advocates to survivors. Typically these are fellow MST survivors who understand and appreciate the nature of their position, having navigated similar situations themselves. One of the most significant aspects of POD's work is to provide advocacy and legal representation from either their own Legal Center or one of the many pro bono attorneys they work with across the country. Finally, POD assists individuals with obtaining appropriate veteran benefits.

One of the most important aspects of POD's work is its advocacy efforts. POD's out-front public advocacy works tirelessly to get injustices covered in the media and in front of senior military leaders and Congress. In this manner, they apply pressure to key decision makers to help drive change. They have been successful working with various media to get their message and survivor stories out. POD has participated in various documentaries with organizations such as CNN, Vice, and Univision, highlighting sexual violence within the military. According to Christensen, all major reforms resulted from POD pointing out injustices and bringing them to the media and to Congress.

"We basically embarrassed the military into action," he told me. "Military failures or scandals are what moves the ball ahead, as the scandals evolve into reform." About Vanessa Guillén, he says: "The callous disregard exhibited in that case exposed so much and really showed the failures and evaporated the mystique of the military." Several reviews, to include an independent review, pointed out the permissive environment that existed at Fort Hood for sexual assault and sexual harassment.

The hashtag #IAmVanessaGuillen, created by one of POD's advocates who is herself an MST survivor (see Chapter 14), really propelled the story forward. Christensen believes that the hashtag, the sheer perseverance of Vanessa's family, several key legislators, and the thousands of supporters and survivors across the country who rose up, all culminated in helping push through real reform. "It was the last hurdle for legislative changes to be passed and for transformative reform," he remarks.

Christensen indicates that POD has far more demand than capacity. They rely on many volunteers and collaborators to help survivors. He hopes that, as more hear about Parrish and POD's efforts on behalf of survivors, funding can increase to position POD to be able to fully support the approximately 300-500 survivors that reach out to them annually.

The team at POD has always tried hard to get survivor stories out, to garner congressional support for their recommendations to reform the military justice system, and to showcase how to properly maintain survivors' dignity throughout the sometimes lengthy process of seeking justice. However, it often feels as if they are David in the biblical tale of David and Goliath. "POD is a small organization with a limited budget that is taking on a large organization that has the world's largest budget," Christensen points out, referring to the Department of Defense.

It helps that POD's mission is clear: to end sexual violence, victim retaliation, misogyny, sexual prejudice, and racism in the military, and to combat a culture that has allowed all this to persist. It also helps that they put survivors and those who have experienced injustice first, above any system or infrastructure. You might say that POD has the survivors' six.

Christensen is quite proud of POD's research and subsequent report titled *Racial Disparity in Military Justice*. Their analysis pointed out that throughout all services, Black service members were substantially more likely than white members to face military justice or disciplinary action. POD provided data to show that the disparities did not improve, and in fact has increased in more years.[1]

POD's website is chock full of substantial data. An annual report is produced each year. Their research and fact sheets are quite informative, and their legislative and policy achievements benefit survivors and supporters alike. Much of their data is derived from DoD. There are multiple survivor stories featured, and one particular video on knowing your rights is especially well done. The importance of this cannot be overstated, as many survivors are not aware of their rights or what is even possible regarding support for them.

POD's work is vast, but its staff, volunteers, and pro bono attorneys try but simply cannot meet the demand that exists. So, how can people assist POD in its efforts?

- Become an advocate. If you are a survivor you can serve as an advocate, speak with survivors as they navigate their cases, attend trials, share experiences, and act similar to a sponsor.

- Become an ally. Know what POD can do for survivors and tell others, spread the word, and support their social media and advocacy campaigns.

- Share your story. It can be difficult for people to come forward and speak openly. Recent stories are always helpful.

- Contact your congressional representative. Let them know about MST, make them aware of the issue within the military, and ask for their support.

---

1 See www.protectourdefenders.com/disparity.

- If you're able, donate to the cause. Host fundraising campaigns.

Finally, please go to the POD website for additional information, to become more aware of the support they provide to MST survivors and to those who have suffered racial and sexual injustices. POD remains a major player on the MST Battlefield. It is important that you be educated and aware of their services and programming. MST warriors have a powerful ally and champion in POD.

https://www.protectourdefenders.com/

CHAPTER 16

WHEN TO FIND HELP: SEEKING TREATMENT FOR PTSD

Sandra B. Morissette, PhD

There are multiple ways to seek healing following trauma, and there is no one right way to do that, as everyone is different. For example, many of the people in this book have never before told their truth, and for some, simply telling their story can be an important way to heal and find their voice in what is often the silence of trauma. Others will express themselves through journaling, painting, music, or the listening ear of a supportive friend. Yet others will opt to seek professional help, which is the focus of this chapter.

One of the hardest and most important steps following MST is determining whether or not one needs professional help, how to find help, and what treatments we know work best. Notably, although post-traumatic stress disorder (PTSD) is one outcome following trauma, it is not the only outcome. Some might struggle with other conditions, such as depression, anxiety disorders, eating disorders, or addictive behaviors. Importantly, there is no need to self-diagnose. Rather, a trained mental health provider can conduct an assessment and provide recommendations for treatment as needed. Below are a few considerations to think about in the path to seeking professional help for PTSD.

What is PTSD?

Not everyone will develop PTSD following trauma, but for those who do it is important to recognize the signs and symptoms. The American Psychiatric Association (APA, 2013) has defined PTSD as occurring in response to experiencing or witnessing a life-threatening event, including sexual assault, but also including combat, natural disasters, car accidents, or other such events. Sometimes people will have experienced more than one type of event. Symptoms of PTSD include reliving the event (e.g., intense memories, nightmares), avoiding reminders of what happened (e.g., avoiding people, places, or things that bring back memories), having increased negative thoughts and feelings that are different than before the traumatic event (e.g., feeling numb or unable to have positive feelings), and hyperarousal (e.g., feeling irritable, difficulty sleeping or concentrating, engaging in reckless behaviors). Importantly, it is normal to have many of these symptoms immediately following an event. However, if the symptoms last more than a month *and* are upsetting to the person or cause work, home, or social problems, then a diagnosis of PTSD should be considered.

How do I know if I need treatment?

There is a culture in the military around not seeking help, because of concerns it could show "weakness." Because of this, determining whether one needs professional help can be a hard, yet critical step. The main question to ask oneself is: Are the symptoms I'm experiencing causing *significant distress or problems* in my life? Think about family functioning, work functioning, completing day-to-day activities, social life with friends, community engagement, or other areas that are important to you. If the answer is yes, and you realize that the coping strategies you've been using are no longer helping, then treatment could be a good option. Importantly, there is no reason to struggle on your own. And, finding an expert who can help you could *shorten* the time to your recovery and get you back on the path to leading the life you want to be leading.

How do I find help?

Getting connected to treatment is not always easy, so prepare yourself to do some information gathering and legwork. It is important to find a therapist with the right expertise and training in treating PTSD and understanding military culture. You may need to contact more than one resource, and even try more than one therapist, to find the right fit. If going through insurance, it is also important to find a therapist that takes your insurance, so that the costs of therapy do not become a burden and stressor.

It is beyond the scope of this chapter to list out all resources, so a few places to start are highlighted here. Some military and veterans may feel comfortable with and choose to go through the military (e.g., Tricare) or the Veterans Health Administration. Military personnel can reach out for help through Military One Source (militaryonesource.mil), and veterans can also find information online about VA facilities, mental health treatments, and benefits (mentalhealth.va.gov). Other good sources to reach out could be a trusted friend who is connected with either system, or seeking private care.

Some service members and veterans may have lost trust in these systems by virtue of their trauma, and will choose treatment through the private sector. Outside of military systems, one option may be the Cohen Veterans Network (cohenveteransnetwork.org), which is growing in their locations around the United States. They provide evidence-based mental health treatments to veterans, military, National Guard and Reserves, and their family members. Of course there are numerous other providers, and an internet search in your area is advisable, keeping in mind that some programs do accept patients from out of state. For example, Emory Healthcare Veterans Program offers a free PTSD treatment program (including travel, lodging, and meals) to post-9/11 veterans and service members (https://www.emory-healthcare.org/centers-programs/veterans-program/index.html). This is just one example, and there are many others.

What treatments work for PTSD?

Before getting into the specific treatments, it is important to consider a phenomenon that some experts in the field call the "paradox of avoidance." Avoidance is a very common experience in response to traumatic events, and is in fact part of the symptom criteria for PTSD. In order to cope with what happened, many people avoid having thoughts and emotions related to the trauma, or doing things that remind them of the trauma (e.g., watching the news or a movie, or avoiding situations, people, or places that trigger memories). Although this can provide short-term relief, paradoxically, trying not to think about what happened does not help to resolve PTSD symptoms over the long term. By contrast, although asking people to think about their thoughts, memories, and feelings can feel very scary, facing memories is often a critical part of the recovery process and a key element of treatment. This means that you may need to overcome the urge to avoid even when seeking treatment. What is important to remember is that mental health providers work carefully with patients to systematically think through their memories of what happened in a safe, therapeutic context.

The good news is that there are several trauma-focused psychotherapies that are effective for treating PTSD. Below, six of the most common psychological treatments for PTSD are briefly described. The first three have the strongest evidence base to date, but the other three also have evidence and are recommended treatments. Deciding which treatment is best for you can be based on any number of factors, including personal preference and availability of a therapist trained in using a particular treatment. Providers and patients should have a collaborative discussion about what treatments are available and which might be in the patient's best interest.

Prolonged Exposure (PE; Foa & Rothbaum, 1998). PE is an individual treatment that typically lasts 8-15 sessions. PE helps patients to progressively think about trauma memories, feelings, and situations that remind them of the situation. Patients are guided in the sessions to use imaginal exposure, which is a process that involves describing the event out loud and in detail. The therapist and patient then talk about their reactions, including any thoughts and emotions they experienced. By thinking and talking about the traumatic event, the patient learns that the memories are not dangerous and do not need to be avoided. Outside of sessions, the patient also learns to systematically confront triggers (people, places, situations) that remind them of the traumatic event.

Cognitive Processing Therapy (CPT; Resick, Monson & Chard, 2016). CPT generally lasts 12-18 sessions and can be delivered in group or individual format. Originally developed for sexual assault survivors, group treatment can help patients feel less alone in their experiences. CPT focuses on the relationship between thoughts and emotions, and the therapist asks the patient questions about "stuck point" thoughts (e.g., guilt, self-blame about what happened). Stuck points are statements about oneself, others, or the world that are generally extreme beliefs that are negative in nature and believed to prevent recovery. The therapist works with the patient to create more balanced, realistic thoughts about what happened. Treatment also involves practicing cognitive strategies in between sessions.

Specific Cognitive Behavioral Treatments for PTSD (CBT; Monson & Scnaider, 2014). Session length can vary based on the type of CBT used, but is typically around 12 sessions. CBT helps patients to understand how their thoughts, feelings, and behaviors related to trauma influence each other. For example, how one thinks about a situation can influence how they feel and what they do (and vice versa). Patients are taught how to evaluate unhelpful thoughts and beliefs and develop more balanced thoughts. As with PE, exposure to traumatic memories and reminders is used, with the aim of reducing avoidance behaviors. CBT also focuses on managing emotions and stressors.

Eye Movement Desensitization and Reprocessing (EMDR; Shapiro, 2017). EMDR usually occurs twice per week for 6-12 sessions. EMDR attempts to change the way memories are stored in the brain in order to reduce symptoms of PTSD. Patients think about their traumatic experience while the therapist engages bilateral stimulation of the brain by using either eye movements or other rhythmic patterns (e.g., tones or taps).

Written Exposure Therapy (WET; Sloan & Marx, 2019). WET lasts five (5) sessions and involves writing about the traumatic event in a detailed manner. Patients write about what happened during their traumatic experience, including their deepest thoughts and emotions. Style of writing and grammar are not important, rather what is important is the level of detail in the writing.

Brief Eclectic Psychotherapy (BEP; Gersons, Meewisse, & Nijdam, 2015). BEP is an individual treatment lasting 16 sessions. BEP incorporates

CBT plus other psychodynamic techniques that focus on understanding shame, guilt, and the patient's relationship with the therapist. Patients are encouraged to talk about how the trauma has affected them and their view of the world.

What's next?

If you think you need help, seeking treatment for PTSD is a critical first step and shows strength and courage. There is no need to struggle alone, and social support can be a vital aspect of recovery, whether from a therapist, family, or friends. This chapter provides a brief overview of recommended treatments, and therapists can guide you in understanding your treatment options and what is best for you. In the military, when a problem or challenge occurs, an action plan is developed and executed. Why not create a plan for yourself? You are your most important mission.

References

American Psychiatric Association. Task Force on DSM-V (2013). *Diagnostic and statistical manual of mental disorders: DSM-5* (5th, text revision. ed.). American Psychiatric Association.

Gersons, P. R. B., Meewisse, M., & Nijdam, M. J. (2015). Brief Eclectic Psychotherapy for PTSD. In Schnyder, U. & Cloitre, M. (Eds.) *Evidence-based treatments for trauma-related psychological disorders.* Switzerland: Springer International Publishing

Foa, E. B., & Rothbaum, B. O. (1998). *Treating the trauma of rape: Cognitive-behavioral therapy for PTSD.* Guilford Press.

Monson, C. M. & Shnaider, P. (2014). *Treating PTSD with cognitive-behavioral therapies: Interventions that work.* Washington, DC: American Psychological Association.

Resick, P. A., Monson, C. M., & Chard, K. M. (2016). *Cognitive processing therapy for PTSD: A comprehensive manual.* New York, NY: Guilford Press.

Shapiro, F. (2017). *Eye movement desensitization and reprocessing (EMDR) therapy: Basic principles, protocols and procedures.* (3rd ed.). New York, NY: Guilford Press.

Sloan, D. M., & Marx, B. P. (2019). Written Exposure Therapy for PTSD: A Brief Treatment Approach for Mental Health Professionals. Washington, DC: American Psychological Association.

Sandra B. Morissette, PhD

Dr. Morissette is a Professor at The University of Texas at San Antonio (UTSA), and Chair of the Department of Psychology. She received her PhD in clinical psychology from Boston University and is a Fellow of the American Psychological Association, Division 56 (Trauma Psychology). Prior to coming to UTSA, she completed her training and worked in the Veterans Administration for over 18 years, most recently serving as the Treatment Core Chief of the VA VISN 17 Center of Excellence for Research on Returning War Veterans. In 2015, she became the Director of the Trauma Health Research In Veterans' Experiences (THRIVE) laboratory at UTSA.

Her expertise is in studying co-occurring conditions, including trauma/PTSD, anxiety disorders, and addictive behaviors, with a particular interest in understanding factors that affect functional recovery in post-9/11 veterans as well as suicide prevention. Dr. Morissette's research has been funded by the Department of Veterans Affairs, Department of Defense, and National Institutes of Health. She has published over 100 peer-reviewed articles and book chapters, and serves as a Consulting Editor for the *Journal of Clinical Psychology*. She enjoys mentoring undergraduate and graduate students, as well as teaching Military Health Psychology and Introduction to Clinical Psychology.

Afterword

This book was not a labor of love. It was a gut-wrenching, painful deep dive into my past military service, often difficult to withstand or comprehend what I had actually endured. It was the same for the thirteen courageous souls who accompanied me on this journey. They too, reached back into the dark recesses of their minds to reflect on their own experiences. For some of us it went back many years, for others just a few, and for two, who are currently living their active-duty service, it was real time. It hurt deeply, we commiserated, we cried, but we also laughed and marveled at our newfound strength in sharing our truths.

Many of the stories you have just read have never been told before or in such detail. I know how hard it must have been to read through each one, especially for our families, friends, and fellow service members who might never have been aware of the depths of our suffering. Imagine what it was like for us to live these experiences, day in and day out over days, months, or years. Many of us never shared with anyone our lived experiences or how much we had been affected by them. Now you know what it was really like for us as we navigated the more negative aspects while serving our country.

MST happens to anyone and everyone. It does not discriminate. We are your sisters, brothers, daughters, sons, fathers, mothers, grandmothers, grandfathers, everybody. We represent the faces behind MST: those who spoke up, those who didn't, and those who cannot speak up because they are no longer with us. You know us. You just didn't know our stories. Now you do.

I wanted to put a face on MST, to personalize it for readers and let other survivors and their families know they're not alone. The more I spoke with survivors, the more determined I was to tell their stories. I wanted you to *know* these MST warriors, to learn the up close and personal reality of their experiences, to get an insider's viewpoint. I also wanted to show the similarities that ran across all the stories. And I wanted to convey the ineffectiveness of previous military policies like zero tolerance. Failed policies and inept leadership allowed MST to remain endemic throughout the military. Leaders were not held accountable. Our military history cannot exclude these powerful stories of MST experiences. They must be included so we can learn and not repeat the insanity of past approaches.

When I decided to write these stories, it was important to me to capture a wide range of those affected by MST. The breadth of those I selected to write about spanned decades as well as all branches of the military, officer and enlisted personnel, racial, ethnic, gender, and sexual orientation diversity, as well as a variety of combat and overseas assignments. I also wanted to begin and end the book with my own poetry that could speak authentically to my journey regarding MST.

I never spoke about my own MST to anyone until recently. Not to my spouse at the time, my son, or any of my family or best friends. I didn't bring it up upon my military retirement in 2010, or for ten years after. When asked I would comment on sexual harassment, sexism, disparities I felt as a woman and a Latina, but I never spoke up about being sexually assaulted in initial training or about the true extent of my sexual harassment experiences.

It was in an op-ed article I published in November 2020, following the horrific murder of Vanessa Guillén at Fort Hood, that I first spoke up. When I saw her face, I saw my own face at twenty-one. It was as if I had been sucker punched. Her murder sparked repressed memories that I could no longer deny. All the buried toxicity and trauma reared its ugly head and began demanding to be let out. A dam had broken, memories flooded in, and I was forced to reflect and confront them. It was ugly and maddening to face my demons.

Jumping into what I call the abyss, I felt shame, guilt, and rage. I began a truth-seeking journey of reflection, battling monsters, and finally acknowledging what had happened to me. I could no longer run from my pain; it was at the front door screaming to be let in and addressed. It was at this point that I decided that I wanted to heal the deeply buried wounds of combat and MST.

I was glad that during 2020 and early 2021 no one was with me, as I hunkered down, self-isolating during the pandemic. I followed the op-ed with a deeply personal poem in April 2021, using the coronavirus as an analogy to convey the hidden secret of my MST. I titled the poem "Into the Light" and placed it at the start of this book. I wrote it because I had to. The words kept dancing around inside my head, then came bursting out in the form of poetry. My years of being silent on the issue were forever over; there was no going back.

Several former military members were stunned when I shared the poem. They had never seen the vulnerable colonel, only this *chingona* who had never shown weakness or fear. I had built up such a solid steel wall around me for so long that even I was shocked and unprepared as the steel began slowly to melt away.

So many people related to my op-ed and poem. I was surprised at how many reached out and trusted me enough to start sharing their stories. I knew that, if I could capture some of their MST stories, it could contribute to a national dialogue and the momentum that was building to demand change within the ranks. I also wanted to help educate the public about the far-reaching impacts of MST. I didn't have to put out a call asking for people to participate; they all just found me. Some were colleagues or friends that I had no idea had experienced MST.

Many used my own words from either the op-ed or the poem when they contacted me offering and asking to be part of the "No Más" movement for change. I became overwhelmed with all the people contacting me. Their stories became the fuel I needed to channel my anger into writing. I started writing poetry about combat, PTSD, and MST experiences. The words just came flowing out of me. After so many years of being silent, I began speaking up in a big way and felt compelled to write this book. I believe that I have been guided by the Lord on this difficult journey. I am following the path set out for me and am not alone, for he is with me. So are my sisters and brothers who served. I feel them each time I put pen to paper.

Sadly, I could have included many more stories than I did. That is the ugly truth about MST. I strongly believe that the number of those affected is significantly larger than anyone really knows.

Before I interviewed those I selected to be in the book, I wanted to write my own story. I wanted to go through that painful, difficult task before asking others to tell me their stories. It was the commander in me coming out: never asking my troops to do something I wouldn't do. I knew it was going to be traumatic, and I wanted to experience it first.

So I began writing my own story. I would write a few lines, then walk away enraged. There were times I just screamed, until I was spent. Other times, I just cried. I was furious. I was incredulous that it had happened. To me. To the others. It took some time before I began to feel safe again. In fact, I still struggle with this. It took a while for me to control my anger, to accept what had happened and begin therapy to process all my emotions, memories, and pain. The abyss called out to me again and again. I had to fight my way out. I knew I couldn't remain where all that pain existed. If I did, I would be lost forever.

I began to interview the thirteen individuals included in this book, and I listened to their stories without judgment. This proved a difficult task, as some of them had experienced horrific incidents in their childhood and while serving. Sometimes their stories jarred my memories even more, and I began recalling additional details of my own experiences. Occasionally I would comment that what had happened to them had happened to me too. Some were so surprised that I was a full colonel, yet had experienced what they had experienced. I reminded them that most of my MST occurred early in my career when I had no real rank and no agency and was considered irrelevant. I could relate to many in this book, for I had experienced discrimination for being a woman *and* a Latina. I was overwhelmed at how much they shared. I was amazed at how much I shared.

I took seriously my responsibility to honor both their service and their experiences. Each time I began to write one of their stories, I found myself falling back into the abyss and had to crawl my way back out. At times this proved difficult. I became enraged all over again, their stories triggered my own experiences, and I found myself wanting to go back in time to save all of us from what happened.

Writing each experience took its toll on me, both physically and emotionally. After each interview and each story I wrote, I had difficulty leaving behind the pain, trauma, and betrayal. I am a disabled veteran, and my conditions worsened during this time. I wrote this entire book standing up, as my spine issues wouldn't allow me to sit for long periods. I was forced to take more breaks than I had planned, due to pain or triggering memories. Pain is a tough sidekick that kept hitching its ride onto my excursions into the abyss.

The abyss became like a seductive lover, calling me back into the comfort of its embrace. It took sheer willpower to step away, back into the light. It took Latina power, woman power, sister and brother in arms power. Each story detailed in the book provided pain, but also empowerment. My vulnerability became like a wakeup call for the determination to live an authentic life. I was astonished that the vulnerability I was displaying actually provided me immense strength.

As I undergo my healing journey, I am grateful to the VA for their efforts. They have come a long way in providing counseling, care, and programming to MST survivors. My own therapist assisted me as I battled my demons and began to write about the horrific experiences of others. I am no longer ashamed that I need help. Years ago, I never sought out help due to the stigma associated with being a commander and how that might affect me while I was active duty. The military culture must change regarding mental health and self-care. We must be able to get help, still serve, and encounter no retaliation.

Some of us are still undergoing some form of therapy and finding our rightful place after trauma. None of us depicted in this work want your pity. We want only to educate you and make you aware of the tentacles that MST has and the way it imbeds into our lives, tightening its grip at the least expected time, never quite releasing its hold. MST happened to us, but it doesn't define who we are or the potential that remains. Resilience is a powerful theme throughout each story. Our stories, our truths are now captured forever.

It's important for me to say that I love my country, loved serving in uniform, and am proud of my service. In my thirty years of service, I met thousands of military professionals and forged bonds with several of these outstanding individuals, both men and women. I literally went to war with them and trusted them with my life, to have my back as I had theirs. These are the individuals I want to remember when I reflect on my service, the real heroes of my journey, not the MST or the experiences of ethnic disparities. Those remain only a part of my service and speak to the rogue few that were allowed to carry out their dastardly deeds unrestrained.

Now that you have read these stories and have come to know just how deeply entrenched MST is within the ranks and how enduring its impacts are, what will you do with that knowledge? These are lifelong implications for many of us. Will you stand by and remain silent when you witness MST, or will you speak up and demand that people be treated with respect and dignity? Will you hold military leaders at all levels accountable? Will you contact your congressional representative and tell them that this can no longer be tolerated, and that you will be watching to see how the new laws regarding MST within the military will be implemented? Will you do your part to protect all those that served, not just a few?

We are on the brink of a sea change within the military, but these changes are regarding military justice law and do not speak to a change in culture. I believe that the culture change pertaining to MST will take at least another generation to take hold. It probably will not occur until we have more of a critical mass of women and diverse individuals serving *and* in leadership positions. Injustices and disparities throughout the military only prohibit good order and discipline and negatively impact the mission.

Ultimately, this is a leadership issue. I agree wholeheartedly with MG Tony Cucolo, U.S. Army retired, that leaders at all levels must stand up and lead, and not tolerate inequities within the military or within any organization. Human dignity and respect for all must be at the forefront of any policies moving forward.

I never dreamed that I would share my most personal trauma publicly. It went against everything I had been taught, to never show weakness. Doing so now puts me in a vulnerable position, but it also affords me a type of freedom, authenticity, and empowerment that I never experienced previously and is quite liberating. Although it took me years to speak about my experiences, I have faith that doing so now will add to the momentum that began after the murder of Vanessa Guillén and others and will stand in the gap for so many who have not yet found their voice.

I wrote the final poem for this book, "MST Warrior," after I had written all the stories in the book. I wanted to write something to represent the journey I had been on. As I shared it with the others in the book, they told me that it also captured many of their own feelings. They saw their journeys woven throughout the poem. With the telling of our stories, we have formed a strong bond of pain, betrayal, and resilience, a bond forged in trauma.

Lisa Carrington Firmin
San Antonio
April 2022

MST Warrior

by Lisa Carrington Firmin, December 2021

I am a Military Sexual Trauma warrior
Never a victim, much more than a survivor
Owning my past jettisons me into a present and future worthy of happiness.

MST happened to me, without my permission or consent
It didn't matter what I wore, how much I might have drunk
The power differential was huge, I was young, vulnerable, a nobody

Overpowered and betrayed by someone I trusted and respected
A predator took advantage, exploited my weaknesses
with no regard for my humanity

I know now it was about power not sex
MST rests alongside my pain, guilt, and shame, haunting me
But resilience emerges the strongest of them all

Astounded at how many fellow MST Warriors are out there like me
Their strength, courage emboldens me on a journey of healing and advocacy
Can no longer sit idly by, I am compelled to act

MST Warriors everywhere cry out for justice and change
Every lived experience shared brings vulnerability AND empowerment
Our stories are important.
One is powerful; combined they blend like a commanding tsunami

Sharing my story and others to make a difference on the MST Battlefield
Not broken, but beautifully crafted to emerge stronger after trauma
For I am an MST Warrior.

APPENDIX I

Resources and Organizations

The following resources and organizations are just a small sampling that are available for military, veterans and their families when seeking assistance, support, and treatment for MST. This listing is by no means complete. You are encouraged to cast a wide net when seeking resources regarding MST as approaches taken should be tailored to the specific needs of individuals.

Department of Veterans Affairs

- Beyond MST mobile app
  https://mobile.va.gov/app/beyond-mst

- Center for Women Veterans; https://www.va.gov/womenvet/

- Center for Minority Veterans;
  https://www.va.gov/centerforminorityveterans/

- MST overview; treatment, resources and next steps
  https://www.mentalhealth.va.gov/msthome/index.asp

- National Center for PTSD, https://www.ptsd.va.gov/

- PTSD overview; treatment and next steps
  https://www.mentalhealth.va.gov/ptsd/index.asp

- Veterans Crisis Line, available 24/7: Call 1-800-273-8255
  and Press 1, chat live, or text 838255

Department of Defense

- DoD Safe Helpline; call 1-877-995-5247

- DoD Sexual Assault Prevention and Response Office https://www.sapr.mil/

- Military OneSource https://www.militaryonesource.mil

- U.S. Air Force https://www.resilience.af.mil/SAPR/

- U.S. Army https://www.armyresilience.army.mil/sharp/

- U.S. Coast Guard https://www.dcms.uscg.mil/Our-Organization/Assistant-Commandant-for-Human-Resources-CG-1/Health-Safety-and-Work-Life-CG-11/Sexual-Assault-Prevention-Response-and-Recovery-Program/

- U.S. Marines https://www.usmc-mccs.org/index.cfm/services/support/sexual-assault-prevention/

- U.S. Navy https://www.cnic.navy.mil/ffr/family_readiness/fleet_and_family_support_program/sexual_assault_prevention_and_response.html

National, State and Regional

- Birdwell Foundation of San Antonio http://www.birdwellfoundation.org/

- Circle of Arms https://www.circleofarms.org

- The Cohen Center Veterans Clinics https://www.cohenveteransnetwork.org/clinics/

- Emory Healthcare Veterans Program PTSD treatment https://www.emoryhealthcare.org/centers-programs/veterans-program/index.html

- Grace After Fire https://www.graceafterfire.org/about-us

- Michigan Veterans Affairs Agency; https://www.michigan.gov/mvaa

- Military Sisterhood Initiative https://www.challengeamerica.com/msi

- National Alliance on Mental Health, NAMI https://www.nami.org/home

- National Sexual Assault Hotline, 800.656.HOPE

- National Sexual Assault Resources https://www.rainn.org/national-resources-sexual-assault-survivors-and-their-loved-ones

- The Pink Berets https://thepinkberets.org/

- Protect our Defenders https://www.protectourdefenders.com/

- South Texas Research Organizational Network Guiding Studies on Trauma and Resilience https://patriot.uthscsa.edu/strongstar/

- Texas Veterans Commission; https://www.tvc.texas.gov/women-veterans/

- Uniting US https://unitingus.org/

- UTSA Resources for Women Vets https://cmas.utsa.edu/resources/#women

- UTSA Wellbeing Services for Veterans https://www.utsa.edu/students/wellbeing/services/veterans.html

- Veteran Healthy Minds Advisory Council – South Texas https://veteranshealthymindsadvisorycouncilsouthtexas.com/

- Women Injured in Combat: For All Women Veterans (WINC) https://wincforall.com/

- Women Veterans Empowerment & Thriving https://www.womenveteransempowered.org/

- Women Veterans Interactive
  https://womenveteransinteractive.org/

- Women Veterans Network, WoVeN
  https://www.wovenwomenvets.org/

APPENDIX II

Interior Photo Details

Chapter 1: Us vs Her

- U.S. Air Force Officer Trainee Lisa Carrington Firmin, 1980
- U.S. Air Force Colonel Lisa Carrington Firmin, Balad AB, Iraq, 2004

Chapter 2: The Grunt

- Women's Army Corps SP6 (SSgt) Sue Caldwell, Long Binh, Vietnam
- Sue Caldwell, 2021 (photo by Matt Roberts)

Chapter 3: The Shirt

- U.S. Air Force Senior Airman Audrey Magnuson, 1982
- Audrey Magnuson, 2017

Chapter 4: It's a Man's Navy

- U.S. Navy Seaman Recruit JS, 1986
- JS and her pooch Lexie, 2018

Chapter 5: Double Standards

- U.S. Army PFC Jennifer Lugo, Basic Training, 1989

- U.S. AF Major Jennifer Suarez-Lugo, Sadar City, Iraq, 2009

Chapter 6: The Greater Good

- U.S. Coast Guard Radarman 3, Tammy Barlet, 1997

- Tammy Barlet, MPH, 2021

Chapter 7: The Sisterhood

- U.S. Army Private Zaneta Adams, Basic Training,1998

- Zaneta Adams, 2021 (photo by Grand Valley State University)

Chapter 8: Actions Not Words

- U.S. Coast Guard LTJG Denise Rucker, 1999

- Denise Krepp testifying before US Commission on Civil Right, 2019

Chapter 9: Semper Fi

- U.S. Marine Corps Private Stesha Colby-Lynch, Boot Camp, 2006

- Stesha Colby-Lynch, 2021

Chapter 10: Broken Trust

- U.S. Army PFC Victor Gonzalez, Advanced Individual Training, 2010

- Victor Gonzalez, 2018

Chapter 11: Shock and Awe

- U.S. Air Force Second Lieutenant JC Jackson, Air and Space Basic Course, 2011

- U.S. Air Force Captain JC Jackson, Kabul, Afghanistan, 2017

Chapter 12: Triple Threat

- Silhouette (provided by Kait Glasswell)

Chapter 13: Stronger Than Before

- Silhouette (provided by Kait Glasswell)

Chapter 14: #IamVanessaGuillen

- U.S. Army Private Karina Lopez, Basic Training, 2016

- Karina Lopez, 2022

Acknowledgements

There are many to recognize and thank for assisting throughout the process of writing and publishing this book. First and foremost, I must give it up to my Lord and Savior, for leading me on this journey. Second, but so vital to the writing of this book, are the thirteen MST Warriors who bared their souls and shared their stories with me. They deserve so much credit for speaking out. I was honored to write their stories. They truly became my last command, and I am forever grateful to them.

Additionally, my sincerest thanks to:

Major General KC McClain: Your leadership and strength have always meant so much to me. I am deeply indebted to you for the book's foreword.

Dr. Sandra Morissette: Your outstanding contribution of a chapter on seeking support for PTSD enhanced this book and will help others.

Colonel Don Christensen: Your totally selfless support to me and others demonstrates the true servant leader that you are.

All those who served as early readers: Colonel Don Christensen, Lupita Colmenero, Lieutenant Colonel Rick Crosson, Major General Tony Cucolo, Jeff Gatlin, Vanessa Meade, Ginger Miller, Jenny Pacanowski, and Jeb Wyman. Your generosity and the value of the good advice you provided cannot be overstated.

All my brothers and sisters in arms: Your sacrifice to our country will never be forgotten.

UTSA Veteran and Military Affairs, Dr. Michael Logan, William Lansdon, and Reuben Aleman: Your unwavering support fuels me to do everything I can to help my fellow vets.

TAMUK: Proud to have earned my Journalism degree and garnered a great educational foundation with you all those years ago. The support you provide alumni is noteworthy.

My fellow authors, above all Major General Mari K. Eder for your leadership and spot-on guidance. I was so humbled by other authors who also volunteered their time and expertise to speak with me. And to my new network of Blue Ear Books authors, thanks for welcoming me into the fold and for sharing lessons learned. I am immensely grateful to all of you.

Matt Roberts, my fellow Air Force vet: You do great work and captured a stunning photograph of me for the back cover.

Kait Glasswell, my cover designer: The book's front and back cover designs were awesome and truly captured my early vision.

Jennifer Haywood, my interior designer: I am so thankful for your diligent work to ensure the book came to life and presented so professionally.

My VA EMDR therapist: Your expertise in helping me navigate my combat and MST traumas has been instrumental to keeping me on track and moving forward.

Claudia Tijerina: Your specialized and professional expertise provided much-needed guidance at just the right time in the editing process.

Natalie Khawam: The expertise and encouragement you so generously offered to me were so appreciated. Thanks for leading the pursuit of justice for many.

Dr. Kirsten Gardner: Your willingness to share with me what you learned about writing a book was so like you and helped to narrow my focus. Your selflessness was greatly appreciated.

Debbye Cannon, my sister vet, and sister in Christ, for your unwavering support, encouragement, and review of the entire book in record time.

Ruby Gonzalez, my fellow Javelina and biggest cheerleader: Your enthusiasm and support for the work I do are mucho appreciated.

Phyllis Papa, my dear friend and second mom: Your truly unconditional love and support are forever appreciated. Thanks for enduring my ranting and raving when I had ideas.

Chris Guevara, my college roomie: Your nurturing ways and delicious food sustained me throughout the book process and fed both my body and my soul.

Tish Tamez, the best prima in the world: You are the role model I need, both as a Christian and as a professional leader. Your willingness to brainstorm with me at the drop of a hat helped me in so many ways. Muchisimas gracias por todo.

My extended familia and friends: I am blessed to have all of you in my life providing support. There are too many to list here, but you all know who you are. Proud to count you as my family and friends.

My siblings: You all are amazing. Thanks for allowing me to share a small part of our familia with others, for keeping the faith, and for always supporting me.

My parents: Although you are no longer living amongst us, your presence remains ever present in my life each and every day and I am so grateful for the solid foundation you both provided.

Ethan Casey and Blue Ear Books, my editor and publisher: I needed to find the right person that I could trust to guide me on this difficult and intense journey. You exceeded expectations and became a friend, a colleague, and mentor.

Finally, to my beloved son, I am deeply blessed to have you in my life and appreciate more than you know all your sacrifices growing up as a dependent in the military. For that and so much more, I am eternally grateful. Con mucho cariño y amor.

Printed in Great Britain
by Amazon